The Indigenous Church

Melvin L. Hodges

GOSPEL PUBLISHING HOUSE
Springfield, Missouri
02-0527

THE INDIGENOUS CHURCH

Foreword

It is with great pleasure that I write this foreword to the new, enlarged edition of *The Indigenous Church* by Dr. Melvin Hodges. In its previous editions this volume has received widespread attention from people interested in the science of missiology.

The Indigenous Church has been widely used since it was first introduced in 1953. A standard reference book wherever men seek to implement the New Testament pattern of church development, it provides a simple and workable theology on the place and importance of the local unit of the body of Christ. Its companion book, *Build My Church*, addressed to National church leaders, has been translated into more than a dozen languages.

The author was for 18 years a grass roots missionary in Central America. After that he served two decades in the administrative capacity of field secretary for Latin America and the West Indies in the Division of Foreign Missions of the Assemblies of God. Since his retirement from the latter office he has continued active as a professor in the Assemblies of God Graduate School of Theology and Missions. Here his gifts as a teacher and writer bless his students, and his lectures are among the most popular in the curricular offerings of the school.

I heartily endorse this new edition of *The Indigenous Church*, a book that has already established itself in the reference material of mission science. And I recommend its author who on the anvil of practical experience has worked out the principles he now teaches in the classroom. The ideas expressed in this new, enlarged *The Indigenous Church* will benefit other generations of missionaries and assist them in applying basic Bible principles to their endeavors.

J. PHILIP HOGAN
Executive Director, Foreign Missions
General Council of the Assemblies of God

Preface To First Edition

In presenting a new book on the subject of indigenous church principles, the author makes no claim to originality. Students of missions have analyzed with penetrating acumen our present-day missionary methods and have called for a return to the indigenous principle as found in the New Testament. Why then another volume? Simply this, that although the average missionary may have read some excellent books on the subject, yet he still feels somewhat at sea when he comes to the actual, practical application of the indigenous method.

The essence of this volume was given first in the form of lectures to a group of missionaries at a missionary seminar. Some of those present expressed their desire to have the talks published in permanent form. "We have read books on the subject of the indigenous church, but this is the first time we have heard just how to go about the actual founding of it," was the comment of one missionary. On another occasion a young man ready to leave for the mission field for the first time said to the writer, "I need someone to tell me how to go about my task. What am I to do first, and what will be my second step?" It is in response to this need that the present volume has been prepared.

It may be objected: If the church is to be indigenous, it must develop along its own lines. Therefore any set plan of procedure that the missionary may bring to his work will be of no use, and may be an actual hindrance. This would be a valid objection if the purpose were to impose a set of rules on the church or to regiment its growth. The pattern presented in this volume is suggestive rather than mandatory, and its purpose is to aid the missionary to proceed along right lines and avoid crippling errors. The reader will find that ample room is given for the development of the church along its own national lines; in fact, the whole purpose of the book is to help the missionary to assist the church in doing so.

The reader's indulgence is begged in regard to the recurrent references made to the work in Central America. There is no desire on the part of the author to impose the Central American pattern on other fields. We have drawn many of the illustrations from that field, since it is the area with which we are most familiar. There we have had the opportunity of seeing the indigenous church in all of its major essential stages of development. Then, too, each Republic has its own distinct national characteristics and idiosyncrasies. Thus we have been permitted to see the application of indigenous principles under a wider variety of conditions than would otherwise have been possible.

As to literacy, the population is approximately 80 percent illiterate in the rural districts and 50 percent literate in the cities. This percentage may vary considerably from the higher literacy rate of the cities in Costa Rica to the lower average among the Indian population in the rural sections of Guatemala.

As a textbook for the study of missionary methods by prospective missionaries, as a guide to the first-term missionary, and as a reference book for the more experienced worker, we send forth this volume with the prayer that it shall make some contribution to the ministry of our missionary colaborers engaged in the glorious task of building the Church of Jesus Christ the world around.

MLH

Contents

1

The Goal of Missions— a New Testament Church

Today there are more Christian missionaries working in more countries of the world than at any previous period in the history of the church. They are
also engaged in more diverse activities. Along with
the evangelistic and church-planting ministries are
those auxiliary activities of reducing languages to
written form, the translating of the Scriptures and
training of national pastors and evangelists. There
are also a host of other activities not directly related
to the evangelistic, church-planting ministry, which
include the establishing of hospitals and secular
schools, agricultural projects and industrial schools.

It would be logical to suppose that all the different aspects of the outreach of the church in foreign
lands would be united by a common goal. Yet, what
a variety of answers would be evoked were we to ask
missionaries of the Christian faith throughout the
world to define their goal! Some might reply that
they are endeavoring to Christianize people and better the social conditions so that everyone will be
happier and healthier. Others might answer that their
purpose is to save souls, and still others to witness to
every creature so that Christ's return will be has-
tened. All of these are worthy objectives, but none is
really adequate. Our ultimate goal and the means
which we employ to reach the goal are intricately related. If our goal is not clearly defined we may err

in the choice of methods employed and fail to realize
the true fruit of our labors.

Jesus announced His purpose: "I will build my
church." The apostle Paul states that Jesus loved the
church and gave himself for it. He himself throughout his epistles describes his own labors as being for
the sake of the church. We can have no better goal
than the one set forth in the New Testament. We
would therefore define our objective in this way: We
desire to establish in the country of our labors a strong
church patterned after the New Testament example.
Further, we believe that in order to have a New Testament church, we must follow New Testament
methods.

The following illustration will emphasize the importance of a well-defined goal. Some years ago certain missionaries were sent to the foreign field by a
group interested primarily in giving the Christian
witness to all the earth. They based their objective
and methods on the statement that Jesus had made
that this gospel must be preached to all nations for
a witness. Desiring to hasten the return of the Lord
and realizing that the Great Commission must be fulfilled before that time, they decided that the missionary should not tarry in any one place for an extended
time but rather push on from city to city and give
each place the gospel witness. Little effort was made
to conserve the results. The converts were not formed
into churches nor given the teaching necessary for
them to carry on in church life. As a consequence,
after years of effort and laborious toil, very little permanent results of their labor remained. They had
preached over a wide area but churches had not been
established. They failed to take into consideration,
that though evangelism is important, the ultimate objective of evangelism is the calling out of a people
for the Lord Jesus Christ. The church itself is God's
agent for evangelism. Later on this missionary group

restudied the situation and changed its methods to conform to the long-range objective of the establishing of the church of Jesus Christ.

When the social betterment of the populace has been the principal objective of a mission, the tendency usually has been toward developing institutions such as schools, hospitals, and agricultural projects. These are all worthy projects and the social betterment of a populace is the desire of every Christian. However, according to the New Testament plan these are by-products rather than the heart of the missionary program. When we fail to see this, we build strong institutions but usually the church itself remains weak. Our observation leads us to believe that when the emphasis is primarily on this type of work, the church is left unprepared to meet a crisis, such as a Communist invasion of the country, which forces the withdrawal of foreign funds and personnel. Left without the crutches of foreign aid, on which she has long been accustomed to depend, she cannot stand alone, and the institutions themselves have succumbed to the enemy. It is the indigenous New Testament church that has been better able to survive under such conditions.

Let us examine the elements in this New Testament church that we propose to establish. A careful study of the Book of Acts and the epistles reveals the methods employed by the apostles, and particularly by the apostle Paul, the model missionary, as he went forth and preached the gospel to the Jew and to the Gentile. After preaching the gospel in a city, the converts were brought together in a convenient meeting place, often the home of a believer, and other times in any public location that might be available to them, such as a synagogue or a school. These groups of believers would meet together at regular intervals for worship and instruction in Christian doctrine and conduct. Elders and deacons were chosen from among the

Character- istics of the New Testament Church

number to provide the necessary leadership and ministry as they witnessed to their townspeople and the surrounding area. For example, Paul was in Thessalonica only a few weeks, yet he left a church established in that place. He labored in Ephesus for two years, teaching in the school of Tyrannus. As a result, all the province of Asia in Asia Minor heard the Word of the Lord. His farewell discourse to the Ephesian elders is a classic on the relationship of a missionary to the church which he has founded (see Acts 19,20). The apostle stayed a limited time in one area but he left behind him a church that could govern itself; that could finance its own expenses and that extended the gospel throughout the region. Paul evidently made no appeals for workers from Jerusalem or Antioch to fill the pastorates of the churches which he raised up. And there is no financial appeal made either to Antioch or Jerusalem for support for workers or for the erection of church buildings as far as the record shows. Rather, we find the apostle taking up offerings among these new missionary churches to help the saints of the mother church in Jerusalem when that region was stricken with famine. What a commentary on the effectiveness of the New Testament methods; how far we have drifted from that ideal in our present procedure!

The New Testament church then was first, self-propagating; that is, it had within it sufficient vitality so that it could extend throughout the region and neighboring regions by its own efforts. It produced its own workers and the work was spread abroad by the effort of the Christians themselves. Second, it was self-governing; that is, it was governed by men who were raised up by the Holy Spirit from among the converts in the locality. Third, it was self-supporting; it did not depend on foreign money in order to meet the expenses of the work.

In view of the fact that the New Testament

churches were not dependent on workers or funds from a foreign field but were self-sufficient as local units, what could be said of a church today which must depend upon such foreign help in order to continue to exist? We have known of churches on a mission field which have been established for more than 20 years, with fairly large congregations, which are still unable to support their own pastors. We have heard of a church which after several decades of existence, appealed to the mission board for a new missionary pastor when the retiring pastor was forced to leave the work because of the infirmities of old age. It seems evident that a church that must follow such a procedure is far from the New Testament pattern.

Let us ask ourselves a more searching question. In what condition would we find our work if the mission, because of some emergency, found it necessary to call home its missionaries and cut off funds for the support of our work? Would it be a mortal blow to our church or would our church be able to survive? This is not an idle question since in recent years mission fields have been closed to the missionary for one reason or another. Foreign funds have been withdrawn. The church must be built in such a way that the gates of hell shall not prevail against her. In one field the sponsoring mission passed through a financial crisis and was forced to radically cut funds going to the support of pastors. As a result, pastors failed to find means of support and they left their churches and took secular employment. Abandoned chapels and scattered congregations were the result. It is difficult to escape the conclusion that there was something fundamentally wrong in the life of that church. Surely God does not intend for the church in any country to be so dependent upon a sponsoring foreign mission that when its help is removed the young church sickens and dies.

**The Goal Is
Obtainable**

It is possible to obtain the ideal of a church patterned after the New Testament model. This is possible because the gospel has not changed. We serve the same God and His Holy Spirit is with us as He was with the church in the New Testament times. We do not propose to introduce a new pattern or system. We desire simply to return to the New Testament pattern and see a church founded that will bear the characteristics of the apostolic model. We believe that this is possible because the gospel is universal and adaptable to every climate and race, and to every social and economic level. New Testament preaching and practice will produce a New Testament church in any place where the gospel is preached. People of other lands can be converted and empowered by the Holy Spirit to carry on the work of the church equally as well as Americans or Europeans. The gospel has been designed by God himself, so it fills the need of the African, the Chinese, or the Indian. As a result, there is no place on earth where, if the gospel seed be properly planted, it will not produce an indigenous church. The Holy Spirit can work in one country as well as in another. To proceed on the assumption that the infant church in any land must always be cared for and provided for by the mother mission is an unconscious insult to the people that we endeavor to serve, and is evidence of lack of faith in God and in the power of His gospel.

RETHINK THIS CHAPTER

1. Mention some objectives that are given as the goal of missions.
2. Define the New Testament goal of missions.
3. What has been the result when social betterment becomes the goal of missions?
4. State the characteristics of the New Testament church.
5. Show why the goal of an indigenous New Testament church is obtainable.

2

The New Testament Church— a Responsible Church

We have seen that the New Testament church is a powerful, vital organism with power not only to maintain itself, but to expand and extend itself throughout the country where it has been planted. Yet, we are brought face-to-face with the fact that too often the churches planted by missionaries on foreign fields are not that kind of church. Why the difference? In some places missionaries have labored for fifty years and still the local congregation is unable to carry on alone.. Why is it that after ten, fifteen, or twenty years of missionary effort in a given area, we must still appeal to the home churches for additional funds and workers?

One missionary writes as follows:

"Why, today, do we have still a weak church organization that after years of growth cannot yet stand alone? Why has this church, after being organized as a Field Council for more than twenty years, not been able to produce the type of national leadership necessary to develop, sustain, and consolidate gains made during periods of revival outpourings? After studying this question for the past ten years, we have come to the conclusion that our problem lies in the *failure to work for an indigenous church*. Unless a church can be taught the necessity of shouldering its own burden and facing its own problems it cannot be expected to develop even with the aid of periodic revival outpourings."

**Why the
Weaknesses in
the National
Church**

George R. Upton, former Secretary for Missions of
the Pentecostal Assemblies of Canada, analyzes the
problem and places the blame directly at the door
of the mission and the missionary:

"Here is a missionary agency sincerely devoted to
assuming a creditable share in world evangelism. Missionary candidates are available. Funds are also available for developing the field in question. Land is purchased, and extensive mission buildings erected; missionary homes, churches, schools, hospitals, dormitories,
dispensaries, etc., begin to appear. Workmen are hired,
provision is made for maintenance of the youth who enter
the various schools. When native workers have been
trained, they are placed on salary from funds available to
the mission from its home office across the seas. The missionary, whose time and energies are fully occupied with
the business management of the vast community, antic-
ipates that here will probably be his home for years to
come, so he provides for those extras which make the plan
comfortable and convenient.

"He is the undisputed master over this establishment.
Funds for workmen, for native teachers and preachers
flow through his hands. He hires or dismisses, at will. If
a native church springs up, it is under his direct supervision. He feels impelled to remain as director of this, his
sphere of influence and operations, as long as he remains
a missionary. When on furlough, he describes the progress
made, the buildings erected, and institutions operating;
the number of workers and Bible women employed, the
number of teachers and scholars in the schools. He presents pictures of the whole project. He may even mention
that beyond are other towns and tribes needing the gospel, and may make an appeal for additional missionaries.

"After fifteen to twenty years of this type of work, he
may wonder why the native church does not show some
signs of standing on its own feet. The workers do not
manifest any initiative. The people do not show any concern for the salvation of their neighbors, nor manifest a
willingness to assume financial responsibility for any phase
of the mission work. He realizes that his removal from the

oversight of the mission would bring the whole project to
a standstill, unless another missionary took over.

"What is the reason for this? Simply the plan he has followed. He has treated the people like irresponsible children. He has led them, thought for them, relieved them
of all financial responsibility for years. He has uninten-
tionally robbed them of those practical processes which
develop strong characters in any walk of life, whether in
Canada or China, whether white or yellow-skinned.

"Actually, he has founded a sort of spiritual hospital,
over which he must be chief nurse as long as it remains.
His life work has become a liability instead of an asset.
He has sown his leadership and domination and provision
of every need, and he has reaped the servitude and mal-
nutrition of a community of underdeveloped spiritual
children. How difficult to avoid this result in a mission
that runs predominantely to institutional development!"

Here is the key to the problem: As missionaries, we
have too often trained the converts in dependence
upon us, rather than in *responsibility*. It may be because we have an overprotectiveness for our converts;
it may be that unconsciously we desire to be the head
and have people look to us as the indispensable man;
it may stem from our lack of faith in the Holy Spirit
to do His work in maturing the converts. But for
whatever reason, the fact remains that weak churches
are often the product of the missionaries' wrong approach to their task. How we long to see vigorous
converts who will testify fearlessly to their neighbors!
How much the spirit of dedication and sacrifice is
needed in order that true leadership will develop!
There is one "pearl of great price" in building the
church, and that is *a sense of responsibility* on the part
of the converts. With it, other things being equal, the
church will prosper. Without it, although we bolster
the church with a thousand foreign props, in the end
it will succumb to the inertia and resistance of the
world around. Only God can produce this sense of

responsibility, but the way in which the missionary approaches his task will open or close the door of possibility to this vigorous aspect of Christian living. Here are some things that the missionary must watch.

First, the missionary should have a clear concept of his own work as a missionary and of his proper relationship to the converts. He must understand the transitory aspect of the missionary's ministry in any one area. It has been aptly compared to the scaffolding used in the erection of a building. What would one think of a carpenter if he had to leave the scaffolding up so that the building would not fall down! A missionary may center the work too completely in his own person, in the money that he brings to the work, and in his own abilities. He becomes the indispensable man. The nationals learn to depend on him for everything. Consequently they do not develop initiative and the work never reaches the stage where it can be left without missionary supervision. The successful missionary is one who has done his work so well that he is no longer needed in that area. He can leave the work to his converts. "A modern missionary . . . is not intended to be a permanent factor in the life of an alien people. His work is to make Christ the permanent factor, and himself pass on to other pioneer tasks as quickly as he can. Institutions which tie the foreigner down to permanent work are intrinsically dangerous expedients."[1] The true measure of success is not that which the missionary accomplishes while on the field, but the work that still stands after he has gone.

Is the Mission the Center?

Second, one hindrance may be that the work has been centered in the mission station rather than in the local church. God does not send missionaries out to build mission stations, but to build the church. The

[1]Alexander McLeish, "The Effective Missionary," in Sidney J. W. Clark, *The Indigenous Church*, p. 6.

modern missionary should free himself from the "mission compound" psychology of the past generation. Of course the missionary must have a residence, but the church should be located apart, in the village or city, not on the "compound," and the activities of the converts should center around the church. Workers should be sent out to outstations by the church, and these should be considered as branches of the church rather than of the mission station.

Third, the development of the indigenous church may be hindered by a disproportionate number of missionaries in the area. In order to develop the ability and ministry of the nationals, a missionary should never hold a position which a national is able to fill. When there are too many missionaries in proportion to the number of national workers, the tendency is to let the missionaries fill all the important posts. Thus the nationals are not given proper responsibilities and so fail to develop. Missionary personnel should be so allocated that the missionary will be performing a task that would be left undone if he were not there, and under circumstances that will require him to make use of the nationals in order to meet the demands of the work.

Too Many Missionaries?

A fourth reason for the failure to produce an indigenous church may be found in the missionary's failure to adapt himself to native psychology and methods. An understandable but excessive fondness for the "American way" may make him feel that American methods are the only right methods. The work must be administered according to the American plan, the Bible school patterned after the Bible school program in the United States. Even the chapel must be built according to the American idea of architecture. The nationals find it difficult to fit into this foreign pattern. Therefore, year after year the missionary continues the administration according to his own ideas, and the indigenous church does not develop.

American Methods?

**Too Much
Foreign Money**

Fifth, a frequent hindrance to the development of the indigenous church has been the introduction of foreign funds into the structure of the work, with the result that the church depends on foreign aid for its support and advancement. This weakens the spiritual and moral fiber of the church, kills the initiative of the converts and dulls their sense of responsibility.

Lack of Faith?

Sixth, the missionary may fail to exercise a vigorous faith in God for the development of the spiritual capabilities of his converts. Like a tropical plant in a northern climate, the convert may be placed in a spiritual greenhouse. Sometimes he is separated from his own people and brought to live on the mission compound so he will not slip back into heathenism. The missionary may hesitate to place responsibility upon the shoulders of young converts for fear that they will become discouraged. Perhaps he does not teach them to tithe. Sometimes he fails to take advantage of the new convert's enthusiasm to witness, or has been afraid to allow God-called men to launch out into the ministry, for fear that they would fall into sin. A missionary once said that we could not expect the church on the mission field to take upon itself the ministry of intercession—the converts were too young and inexperienced to understand it!

**Not a De-
pendent Church**

We must found a truly indigenous church on the mission field because the church of Jesus Christ in China, in Latin America or in Africa, is not, or should not be, a branch of the church in America. It must be a church in its own right. We should plant the gospel seed and cultivate it in such a way that it will produce the Chinese or the African church. We must train the national church in independence rather than dependence. A church that must depend on foreigners for its workers, that must call for additional missionaries to extend the work, that must plead for foreign funds in order to keep going, is not an indigenous church. It is a hothouse plant that must have artificial atmosphere and receive special care in order to keep alive. When we find ourselves in a situation like this, let us examine the type of work that we are doing. Let us ascertain why we are building a work that cannot progress without artificial help. Surely the weak thing we have produced is not what Jesus meant when He said, "I will build my church; and the gates of hell shall not prevail against it."

Not only must the missionary have the right concept of his own ministry, but also he must have faith in the power of the gospel to do for others what it has done for us. In the United States, in the early days with hearts aflame, even day laborers went out to preach the gospel. God honored them with ministries and gifts of the Spirit. Now can we have faith in God to do the same for others, regardless of the color of their skin? Or do we disbelieve in His power to work in this manner among other races and in other lands?

RETHINK THIS CHAPTER

1. Why are churches planted by missionaries sometimes unable to assume their true responsibilities?
2. Show the importance of a "sense of responsibility" in the local church.
3. What might be some of the reasons that a church is too dependent on the missionary?
4. Explain how faith on the part of a missionary is important to the founding of a strong national church.

3

Self-government

The three basic elements which make the church indigenous are: self-propagation, self-support and self-government. Should any one of these essential elements be missing, the church is not truly indigenous. We are now to consider *how* the missionary may proceed in order to assure the development of these necessary factors in the national church.

It is usually granted that of these three aspects, self-government is the most difficult to accomplish and requires the longest time for achievement. Yet the principle of self-government is so important and the result in the spiritual life of the church so vital, that if we fail here, it could well mean that we shall fail in the entire program of establishing the indigenous church.

Importance of Self-Government

For this reason we shall consider it first. Self-government makes for a sense of spiritual responsibility which will be reflected in self-support and self-propagation. To fail to place the responsibility of self-government on the converts is to choke their initiative and dwarf their spiritual growth. Furthermore, the rising tide of nationalism in every quarter of the earth demands that the national church be freed from the domination of foreign missionaries. The national converts will doubtless welcome the missionary's leadership in the beginning, but they will not be content for long if the management of the church remains in foreign hands.

If the missionary fails to recognize this legitimate desire for independence, and work along with it, sooner or later dissatisfaction will result. Then an ultranationalistic agitator may come along and the frustration, buried deep in the hearts of the converts because they have not been given their proper place in the work, will come to the surface, and the missionary will have the makings of a division on his hands. The dissatisfied group may even decide that it is necessary to split off in order to be able to govern their own affairs. Many such splits could have been avoided in the past if the proper steps to establish self-government had been taken in time.

"To assume that any native church perpetually requires constant supervision by a missionary is an unintended insult to their capacity to manage their own affairs. The most primitive tribes have some form of local and tribal government, adjusted to existing conditions. Necessity and common sense, even among the most backward and primitive, have so required. How much more then, may those same natives, now washed by the blood of Calvary's Lamb, enlightened with the Word of God, and filled with the Holy Ghost, give wise administration to the church and Community."[*]

Perhaps we had made the mistake of thinking of self-government primarily on a national level rather than in terms of the local church. A national organization in the hands of inexperienced converts would, in the beginning, present almost insurmountable obstacles, but the government of local churches according to the New Testament pattern is not beyond the capacity of the national converts, even though they may be limited as to educational advantages. It is quite evident that there were hundreds of organized local assemblies in the Early Church before the

Self-Government Begins with Local Church

---

[*] George R. Upton in *Indian Witness*.

apostles and elders came together in Jerusalem for the first "General Council." In certain areas, it would appear that we have started at the wrong level.° We have set up an organization at the top level, among missionaries, with perhaps a small number of the most capable workers included, and have hoped that in time organized self-government would filter down to the local church level. In doing this we have started at the wrong place. In order to have any real foundation in self-government, we must begin with the local church. Granted that it may be a slower process, it is nevertheless simpler, and the organizational structure will be laid on a firmer foundation.

Local churches, properly functioning, are the fundamental units of the later, united fellowship. If the missionary is able to organize his converts into local churches, then he has a powerful medium for evangelism and the essential basis for self-government. No matter how many converts there are, or how many workers, if we have not enabled them to form themselves into local, self-governing churches, then we do not have an indigenous church. The first step in self-government then, is the founding of properly organized local churches throughout the district. Any national organization that may exist later, is for the purpose of serving the local churches and aiding in the extension of the work beyond the local sphere.

Necessity of Right Beginning

Since with the establishment of the first local church, we cast the mold for the pattern that subsequent churches are likely to follow, it is of utmost

---

° "It is unwise to organize a Church out of missionaries and their families before there are native Christians, and a presbytery or conference out of foreign missionaries before there are native pastors. . . . Such a policy is apt to force the premature organization of ecclesiastical machinery on the mission field. It creates a church that will always be foreign in spirit. The natives come in one by one and find the foreigners in control, and they regard the whole institution as alien."—A. J. Brown, in *The Foreign Missionary.*

importance that we make a good beginning. Otherwise changes must be made later and changes are difficult. The foundation of self-government should be laid with the first church. If the missionary makes all the decisions at the beginning, the converts will become accustomed to his leadership, and later when they should take the responsibility for the management of their own affairs, he will find that they are unable; even unwilling, to do so. "The temptation (to the missionary) to carry on certain features of the government of the church is almost irresistible. Is the missionary not the father of the church? . . . Therefore, the various items related to the government of the church from the very start have been indicated by the wisdom of the missionary. It is difficult for the nationals to carry on the work independent of the missionary. They have from the start depended on his wisdom and they continue to do so as the church grows. It is only the energy of the Holy Spirit coupled with resistance within the soul of the missionary that will turn over all the factors involved in the government of the church—all its committees, its treasureship, trusteeship, its discipline, its preaching and teaching functions to the nationals. All of it must be by the local members."*

Now for a few suggestions as to practical steps that may be taken to establish a local church on a self-governing basis. Having won a group of converts, the missionary turns from being an evangelist to the function of teacher and instructs them in the precepts of the Christian faith and the standards of Christian living. The Great Commission emphasizes the teaching aspect of the missionary's ministry: "Go ye therefore and TEACH all nations. . . ." The object

---

* From a paper, "A Study of Indigenous Policies and Procedures" prepared by the Conservative Baptist Foreign Mission Society.

of the teaching is to enable the converts to arrive at a clear understanding of Christian faith and conduct.

I think it can be readily seen that there must be a standard of doctrine and conduct accepted in common by the believers, else a true Christian church will not emerge. Every established congregation has some kind of standard, written or unwritten, even including those groups that do not profess to believe in a creed or organization. Their standard may be unwritten, but they have a common understanding and agreement as to points they consider vital.

Agreement on Funda- mentals

To say that the Bible alone is the basis of fellowship is scarcely sufficient, for there is no region, remote though it be, whose isolation provides security from the presence of false teachers. Groups such as the Seventh-day Adventists and Jehovah's Witnesses say that they too are guided by the Bible. Agreement on certain basic points is fundamental to fellowship (1 Cor. 1:10). In the Assemblies of God fellowship, the common basis is our statement of fundamental truths. For example, there is common agreement that a person must be born of God's Spirit before he may become a member of a church. He must also "bring forth fruits" that indicate a true repentance and a genuine experience with God.

The establishing of the Assemblies of God in El Salvador, Central America, will serve to illustrate this point. When our missionary first went there, he found independent groups of believers without church government or discipline. Everyone did that which was right in his own eyes. As could be expected, there were all manner of unhealthy and unscriptural practices and beliefs among the converts.

Some of these converts desired a higher standard of Christian living. These came to the missionary, and together they studied the situation, finally reaching certain conclusions as to standards for church membership. One of the principal decisions was to require legal marriage instead of the common-law marriage or concubinage prevalent in the country. They also decided on church practice and made a statement of basic doctrine. These agreements were published in a little pamphlet with appropriate Scripture references and became the guide for the establishing of local congregations, the exercising of church discipline, etc.° From that beginning the churches made rapid strides in self-propagation, self-support and self-government so that today they comprise the strongest Protestant group in the Republic.°° This could never have resulted if the brethren had failed to reach a basis of agreement.

It is vital that the converts themselves reach an understanding of the Christian life, based on the Scriptures, so that their faith is firmly grounded and they are able to "give an answer to every man that asketh . . . a reason of the hope . . ." 1 Pet. 3:15. Then they are prepared to begin intelligently to work together as a church. It is not absolutely necessary that such an agreement be published in pamphlet form (though the convenience of such a pamphlet can readily be seen); a list of Scripture references under appropriate headings, left on record in the church may suffice.

One point here deserves special emphasis. The standard of doctrine and conduct must be an expression of the converts' own concept of the Christian life as they find it in the Scriptures. It is not enough that it be the missionary's belief. This is a vital distinction. There is nothing to be gained by taking our ideas and forcing them on the converts, as much as to say, "Here is our set of rules. If you are to be a member of our church, this is what you must do."

°See Appendix, page 137.
°See footnote, p. 46.

Instead, we must come together and patiently sit with them, a day or a year, as the occasion requires, until we have reached an understanding. It is to be *their* church, so it must be *their* standard. They are to carry on after we are gone. If it is the missionary's standard and not their own, they will do nothing about it when the missionary is not there to see that it is enforced, but if the truth of the Scriptures has gripped the mind of the convert, then he will feel: "I must do this, not because the missionary says so, but because it is the teaching of God's Word."

Once agreement is reached as to the standard of membership in the proposed church, there follows a second step: the choosing of the charter members. The missionary will request those who desire to become members of the kind of church that they have studied about, to make it known. Then, with the consent of the group, he may choose out three or four of the most dependable and mature converts, requesting them to serve with him as an examining committee.

Charter Members

This committee will review the list of candidates for membership one by one. The candidates will be examined as to their Christian experience, testimony, and faithfulness. The question should be put to the members of the committee: "So-and-so desires to be a member. Should he be accepted?" As the names are mentioned, the missionary should endeavor to arrive at the true opinion of the nationals. This requires patience and tact. Peoples of other lands usually are not noted for their frankness. Sometimes there will be a ready answer, "Oh yes, this man is very sincere and faithful." Again they may be reluctant to express themselves. The missionary may tactfully do a bit of probing. There may be something in the life of the individual of which the missionary is not aware. He may find it wise to leave the committee alone to discuss the matter among themselves for a moment. Perhaps the decision will be that the candidate should wait a little longer and give further proof of his sincerity.

In all this the missionary will be counseling and guiding, but not compelling. He will show them the importance of a good beginning; of keeping the work clean, advising them not to be overanxious for large numbers, or to try to woo the rich and influential. The missionary is laying the foundation and he must proceed with care.

If the committee is in doubt, the missionary should endeavor to guide them by referring to the Holy Scripture. That is an authority that they will honor, and one to which they themselves can appeal. Thus they will see that the authority rests in the Word of God and not with the missionary.

When the list is complete, one of the members of the committee will be appointed to read it to the whole group of converts. If a candidate has not been approved for membership, then in order to avoid offending sensitive natures, it should be pointed out that this is not a denial of membership. It is merely a delay in order to give time for further instruction and Christian growth.

It would be well that the group of converts be given opportunity to express their approval of the work of the committee. They may also ask any question concerning the decisions. When this is done in the right way, the feeling is born in the hearts of the converts that this is truly their church and their responsibility. Therefore it is profitable for the missionary to follow this method, even though he may be perfectly sure that every candidate will be accepted. He is doing more than accepting candidates, he is training the church in self-government.

The next step will be to give Christian baptism to those who have been approved. The question has been asked: Should the missionary baptize the national converts? Obviously he will have to do so at first.

Baptizing Converts

St. Paul baptized when occasion required, but he did not consider it an essential part of his missionary ministry (1 Cor. 1:14-17). The missionary will be wise if he follows the Apostle's example in this. He should insist that as soon as there are recognized national workers, they perform this sacred rite. In the writer's opinion, all recognized pastors should be allowed to baptize their converts and administer the Lord's Supper (in cooperation with the official board). Thus the church will not be deprived of the sacraments so necessary to its growth and spiritual life. Certainly a missionary should not reserve for himself the exclusive right to perform these sacraments after there are recognized national workers. To do so can only weaken the indigenous church and belittle the workers in the eyes of their countrymen.

Following baptism, the names of the candidates should be listed as the charter members of the church. New members will be added from time to time. They will be examined by the church board, with perhaps the guidance of the missionary, at least for the first few times. Our Central American churches hold regular weekly classes for new converts previous to baptism. Ordinarily a continual stream of converts is passing through these classes. It may require from two to three months for them to complete the studies. In the meantime, the majority of the adults must take the necessary steps to meet the requirements of civil marriage. During this period they are introduced into the life and activities of the church. When the day comes for their public baptism, it is indeed a high point in their lives.

Our Central American pastors will not baptize anyone who does not meet the requirements for church membership. "Why," they ask, "should we baptize a man who has no intentions of meeting our standards? We do not want him announcing to outsiders that we have baptized him, if he is not producing the fruit of a convert." Hence all baptized converts are immediately received as members of the church. I do not insist on this point for other fields, but personally I agree with our pastors.

To a casual observer this method of introducing converts into the life of the church and the privileges of membership may seem unnecessarily slow. The object, however, is for them to understand their privileges and responsibilities in becoming part of the church. They must be made to realize the fact that it is *their* church. What a difference this makes!

Now that the church has come into existence, the next step is to provide it with the necessary officials.

The pastor may be chosen first. The missionary will doubtless find it necessary to guide the proceedings by suggestions and counsel, but the decision must rest with the congregation. If a certain worker has been God's instrument in bringing the assembly into being, the choice of the brethren may fall upon him. Or it may be that among the converts themselves there is a man of recognized spiritual leadership— a man whom the others naturally look to and follow. The church may desire him as its pastor. In such a case, he may be regarded as "temporary" pastor to care for the church until a more mature man is available, or until he himself develops in his ministry to the point where he may be recognized as the regular pastor.

Choosing Officials

The election of deacons will follow next. It will be necessary for the missionary to remind the church of the scriptural qualifications required to fill the office of a deacon. The group may wish to name a nominating committee. Under the guidance of the missionary, the committee will then present to the church the names of those eligible to fill the office, so that the church can make its selection from among them.

In several of the Central American republics, the

churches have a rather useful custom. They elect first,
second and third deacons.° Then when the church
is without a regular pastor, or when the pastor is
temporarily absent, deacon number one is in charge.
When deacon number one is absent, deacon number
two takes over. In this way there is no question as
to who should bear the responsibility of leadership.
The deacons are chosen with this thought in mind so
that the more capable men are placed in these positions. On the whole the practice has proved very
satisfactory. Many such deacons have developed
their ministry to such an extent that they have become
full-time workers.

**Providing
Leadership
for new
Groups**

The question may well be asked: Where in a new
work do you find men to fill adequately the office
of deacon? Naturally this is not always possible.
Some sort of government, however is necessary, even
in the newest church,°° so we may fill the gap with a
temporary board. In this case, we make use of the
best material available, but we do not call these men
deacons, but *encargados*, which in Spanish means,
"the ones in charge." This temporary board serves

° This use of the office of deacon doubtless approximates the
ministry of the New Testament *elders* rather than that of deacons;
and to be completely scriptural, probably they should be so designated. However, the principle involved in the practice of deacons
developing a spiritual ministry beyond the "serving of tables" has
the approbation of New Testament precedent in the cases of
Stephen and Philip (Acts 6-8).

°°We believe that we are not far from the apostolic pattern in
providing leadership from among the converts early in the life of the
local church. "According to Ramsay, St. Paul preached in Lystra for
about six months on his first missionary journey, then he ordained
elders and left for about eighteen months. After that he visited
the church for a second time, but spent only a few months in the
province. Then for the last time, after an interval of three years,
he visited them once again, but again he was only a month or two
in the province. From this it is clear that the Churches of Galatia
were really founded and established in the first visit." *From Missionary Methods: St. Paul's or Ours?* by Roland Allen.

until brethren of spiritual maturity develop in the church. Then a regular board should be elected. Such temporary measures are often necessary when a revival sweeps a section. Groups of believers spring up with no experienced workers available. We cannot allow these groups to drift along without leadership. Many such groups have developed splendidly under the leadership of these temporary boards.

The Apostle Paul committed his converts to the care and guidance of the Holy Spirit and to the grace of God. He did not think that it was necessary to continue with them for long periods of time in order to keep them from failure. If we exercise faith in God, He will help both them and us.

If the congregation in question springs up in the same locality where the missionary resides and there is no local pastor, the missionary must exercise special care. He must not continue year after year to make all the decisions for the congregation or do all the preaching. The danger that antagonism may result has already been pointed out.

A second danger should be mentioned: that of spoiling the people so that at a later date they will not be satisfied to accept anyone less than a missionary as their pastor. Compared with the preaching ministry and efficient administration of the missionary, the abilities of an inexperienced national worker are likely to appear quite deficient. To prevent the development of such a situation, the missionary will do well to choose, early in the life of the new church, a deacon or brother who shows promise of usefulness and, with the consent of the congregation, give him at least partial responsibility for the work. The missionary may be able to overcome any reluctance on the part of the believers to accept this arrangement by explaining to them his own responsibility to the other towns and villages of the district. He must point out that he will fail in his mission if he is re-

quired to give all of his time to the care of one church.
When the matter is presented in this light, the converts
will more readily accept the appointed brother as their
pastor, or at least, as copastor with the missionary.

Under this arrangement, it may be necessary for
the missionary to continue his guidance for a time.

**Withdrawal
of
Missionary
from Local
Church**

He will help occasionally with the preaching, but
he should plan to withdraw more and more from
the local affairs until he can leave them entirely in
the hands of the nationals. Frequent, extended trips
into the district will help him to withdraw, and the
converts will become accustomed to the leadership of
the national pastor. Here is where the missionary
should sincerely try "to work himself out of a job."
For he is building a church, and a church must have
its own national pastor to be complete.

As a congregation assumes the responsibility of
self-government, it is important that the national
pastor be shown the steps he should take in order to
maintain good relations with the official board and
congregation, and to promote the efficient administration of the church.

An important step will be the holding of regular
business sessions. The sessions should be held at
least once a month, one with the official board first,
and one with the membership. The pastor should
receive instructions as to procedure in presiding over
the sessions, both as to elementary parliamentary law,
and as to his personal attitude. Thus he may avoid
the pitfalls of profitless discussions and angry tempers.

The private session with the official board may be

**Business
Sessions**

held the week before the general session with the
congregation. A secretary should be instructed to
keep a record of the proceedings in both sessions, and
these minutes should be kept with the church records.
The pastor will preside at the session of the official
board, unless otherwise agreed upon. After prayer,
he will read a list of the matters to be discussed, and

then ask the members of the board if they have any point for discussion that they would like to add to the list. When the agenda is complete, he will present the first point for discussion, and when a decision is reached, will pass on to the next point.

Generally the points to be discussed will include some of the following: Approval of candidates for baptism, cases of discipline when sins have been committed by members of the congregation, counsel and exhortation to brethren requesting advice or needing spiritual help, difficulties that have arisen in the congregation, advance moves planned to benefit the local church. Even though the pastor may not be aware of any special problem, he should call the church board for a session at the regularly appointed time. Often problems exist of which he may not be aware. Should there be no problems, it will still be of great profit to the whole church and enrich the harmony among the leaders, if the time is spent in prayer and intercession for the spiritual progress of the church.

In the general session, the secretary will read the minutes of the previous session, give the financial report and read the decisions of the official board reached in the private session. Candidates approved for baptism and members to receive discipline should be publicly announced. Approval of the action of the board in these cases should be given by voting. Any member should have liberty to ask questions or suggest matters for discussion by the church. The church, by voting, can disapprove of the decisions of the church board, or request reconsideration of a question.

A missionary, when present in a session—and especially if called upon to preside—should encourage correct procedure, but should not be overly insistent on the niceties of parliamentary law. He must be prepared for a considerable amount of informal discussion. He should encourage full and free discussion of all doubtful points in order to arrive at a satisfactory solution. Above all, let his teaching and example emphasize the fact that differences of opinion need not cause a rift in spiritual unity, and that Christians can learn to express their opinions without indulging in carnal and personal feelings.

Responsibility for Discipline

An essential aspect of self-government is the disciplining of members. This is often a difficult and unpleasant task. *Let the missionary beware of acting alone in questions of discipline.* This is a responsibility that should be shared by the entire church. A missionary zealous for the good name of the church, may feel that the question of discipline is too difficult for inexperienced Christians, and decide to act for the church. In following this course, he may attempt to investigate the case; if he finds that the report is true, he may prematurely instruct the secretary to strike the offender's name from the membership list, or restrict his privileges for a certain period.

What is the result of such procedure? Discipline so administered is usually ineffective. The offender has influence; his relatives and friends are members of the church and often they will openly sympathize with him. Officials who carry out the order, nevertheless escape personal responsibility for the act by saying that they are merely carrying out the missionary's instructions. Hence the church does not back up the missionary in his action. The reputation of the church is not cleared nor the offender truly disciplined. For he has not smarted under the disapproval of his fellow Christians. Instead of the church dealing out discipline as a body, the whole affair appears to have degenerated into a personal difference between the offender and the missionary. Consequently, the church lags in spiritual development and becomes less competent to handle such cases. Moreover the good that the missionary hoped to achieve by taking the matter in his own hands, has not resulted, ·since the church has not been purged by true repentance from the leaven of sin that contaminated it.

Yet examples are easily found where churches, left to their own devices, have lapsed into moral indifference and have failed to exercise necessary restraint upon sinning members. What is to be done in such a case? Roland Allen, in *Missionary Methods: St. Paul's or Ours,* presents the case well:

"Nevertheless, when individuals broke through all bounds and committed flagrant offenses he (St. Paul) did not hesitate to insist upon the need of discipline. There is a point at which the conscience of the whole church ought to be stirred to protest, when for the church to pass over an offense in silence is to deny her claim to be a moral society. It is in just such cases that the church is often slow to act. Comparatively small offenses are sometimes visited with stern severity. Horrible crimes shock the whole congregation, but none dares to move.

"Such an offense was committed at Corinth, . . . St. Paul could not avoid moving in the matter, but he obviously did so with great reluctance. It is quite clear that he was determined in the last resort to take action himself, but it is equally clear that he was most anxious to avoid it. He wished the church to realize its responsibility, and to act as a body. . . . He wrote to accuse the church of its failure to realize its duty in the matter. In a case of this kind, according to his view, the church, as a church, had a duty to perform— a duty to the offender and a duty to itself. To shirk that duty was criminal. Therefore he waited to see if the church would do its duty before he interfered himself. In the result, the church did respond to his exhortation, the offender was excommunicated by the majority, he accepted his discipline, he repented, he was restored. . . .

"We look upon the sting of excommunication as exclusion from spiritual privileges; but the man who so acts as to incur excommunication is often the last person to feel that sting. His spiritual apprehension has already been deadened before he falls into sin. What he needs is the public censure of the majority of his fellow-churchmen to awaken his conscience. If the majority of his fellow-churchmen do not avoid him and cast him out, it is little use for a formal sentence of exclusion from church privileges to be issued against him and carried out by officials of the (Mission) society alone. That does no good; it very often only does harm. It hardens the man without humbling or instructing him.

"Moreover, an act of this kind is done not only for the good of the offender, but for the good of the church. It is meant to clear the church's good name which has been sullied by the act of one of its members. . . . But if the majority feel that they have not a real share in the action of the church, if they do not heartily and sincerely realize that the act is their own act, if they consequently do not support it, then there is no real clearance of the church. Nominally the man is excommunicated . . . but if in fact, this has only been the act of a few officials, then in reality there is no clearance. Christians and heathen alike recognize that the leaders of the church have expressed their disapproval. Christians and heathen alike recognize that the body has done nothing of the kind.

"In this case at Corinth we see St. Paul's principle of mutual responsibility again enforced, and he enforced it by staying away from Corinth until the church had realized and executed its duty. . . . St. Paul stirred and educated the conscience of the whole Corinthian church. If he had sent a letter of excommunication to the church, none of those effects would have followed. . . . He threw upon them

Disciplining the Church

the responsibility and trusted to them to learn in what way it was to be fulfilled. In the last resort, he threatened to intervene, if they refused to do their duty, but it was only after he had exercised all his powers to make intervention unnecessary.

"Therefore he succeeded through failure where we often fail through succeeding. We exercise discipline and leave the church undisciplined. He disciplined the church; we discipline individuals. He left the church, and it stood, tottering on its feet, but still standing; we leave the church without any power of standing at all."

In our own experience we have seen very satisfactory results from placing the problems and responsibility of discipline directly upon the church. Rather than this resulting in moral laxity in the church, we have often found that the nationals are inclined to be more rigid in their disciplinary action than we ourselves would have been; so much so, that when we have been called upon for counsel, we have more often found it necessary to stress the need for the spirit of grace in dealing with the offender, rather than to exhort them not to pass lightly over an offense.

Again, the nationals know their own people and have a way of arriving at the facts of a case that would be almost impossible for a foreigner. Thus by making the church itself responsible for the disciplining of its members, the missionary avoids many a costly mistake, and at the same time increases the sense of responsibility among the members.

We have found it to be satisfactory for the official board of the church to serve as an investigating committee. It passes on to the church its recommendation as to the action to be taken. Thus the church as a body acts in the case, pronouncing the disciplinary action without the necessity of scandalous details being made known to immature members.

An unwise custom is followed by some churches who secretly take the name of an offending member off the church roll. This not only lays the pastor or officials open to charges of having been motivated by personal prejudice, but also is completely ineffective in bringing about repentance in the individual concerned, and in clearing the good name of the church. Discipline to be effective must be applied by the majority of the church body. Our experience has been that when it is thus applied, it indeed preserves the norm of the church and often restores the offender.

RETHINK THIS CHAPTER

1. Explain the importance of self-government in the national church.
2. What is the relationship between the rising tide of nationalism and the necessity for self-government in the national church?
3. Where should self-government begin?
4. Explain the importance of organizing the local church if the work is to be indigenous.
5. When should we initiate self-government?
6. What is the first step that the missionary should take in bringing the converts together as a church?
7. How will the church go about reaching an agreement as to standards of doctrine and conduct?
8. How may a missionary go about choosing the charter members of the church?
9. How should the missionary endeavor to keep the nationals from an unwise decision?
10. What procedure may be established for the receiving of new converts into the membership, once the church is established?
11. Why is it important to give the converts a voice in the forming of the church?
12. Who should normally baptize the converts?
13. How are the pastors and deacons to be chosen?
14. What may be done in a new work to establish self-government when the converts are too immature to fill the office of deacon?

15. What dangers are present if the missionary is residing in the same locality where the church is formed?
16. How may the missionary teach the national pastor to maintain good relationships with his church and official board?
17. Explain the procedure in the business sessions of the local church.
18. Who should be responsible for the disciplining of wayward members?
19. In what way may a missionary step in if the church fails to take steps in the disciplining of an offender? How did the Apostle Paul handle this problem?
20. Why is it better for the national church to exercise discipline than for the missionary to settle the matter himself?

4

Self-propagation

Self-propagation is the vital element of the missionary program. It is the true objective of the missionary endeavor. A church which does not propagate itself will soon die out. New Testament churches were self-propagating.

Indigenous church principles recognize the local church unit as the best medium for evangelism. When we have established a local church with all of its rightful and inherent vigor, we have followed God's own method for propagating the gospel.

Every Convert a Witness

Converts are seed—gospel seed. The field is the world, and the seed are the children of the kingdom (Matt. 13:38). Each convert is seed for a potential harvest. By nature, new converts are enthusiastic witnesses. Their vital experience with Christ has made them zealous to impart their newfound knowledge to others. Missionaries must learn to utilize that God-given zeal. It has been said that the Korean Church required each new convert to win someone to Christ before he himself could qualify for baptism. It is vital that each convert be a soul winner.

Putting Converts to Work

Happy is the missionary who has the gift of putting his converts to work. He will see results for his labors far out of proportion to those which follow the labors of a hard-working missionary without this ability.

In this regard many missionaries fail. They insist on personally supervising every move. They are

unwilling to turn the converts loose. These missionaries are always overworked with the visiting of outstations and the conducting of services. While I ad-
mire their zeal and energy, yet I feel that they work
a hardship on themselves and do an injustice to the
work. It has been said that it is better to put ten
men to work than to do the work of ten men. When
the missionary puts the church to work, he not only
gets more accomplished, but the church develops in
the process. Activity and responsibility make for
growth.

We should be careful not to discourage the enthusiasm of a new convert for witnessing by being
overanxious to get everything "under control." Most
missionaries have known of new converts who in
their zeal have gone out, perhaps to their own village,
and won several others by their testimony, sometimes
even before they themselves have been baptized. The
missionary will make a mistake if he sets this zealous
convert to one side in order to send a trained worker
in his stead. A common result is that the work done
by the new convert withers and dies; for the mission-
trained worker is not able to take things on. The
zeal of the convert who has been set aside is likely
to subside, for he has learned that he is not really
capable of being an effective witness. Else why did
the missionary send someone else in his place? Thus
a promising worker is discouraged. The proper step
is to encourage and teach the convert so that he can
develop along the right lines. Roland Allen states:
"We ought never to send a Mission agent to do what
men are already doing on the spot spontaneously."

In Central America, the churches open what they
term *campos blancos*, literally, "whitened fields."
These are outstations, not of the mission station, but
of the church. The churches have an average of two
or three outstations each, and some have as many as
twelve. Each church is considered responsible for the

Evangelism by Extension of the Local Church

evangelization of the surrounding territory, at least halfway to the next church. These outstations have been opened in a simple manner. Perhaps one of the members who lived a considerable distance from the church opened his home for the preaching of the gospel. Or some unconverted person who, for reasons of family ties or previous knowledge of the gospel, was sympathetically disposed, may have desired meetings in his house.

Instead of making these outstations the care of the missionary, the churches appoint their best qualified men to supervise them. They assign a certain lay worker to a given preaching point, making him responsible for that station for a period of time—perhaps for six months. They give him a letter signed by the church officials so that he may avoid trouble with the local authorities. If he is faithful in his task, the church will doubtless permit him to continue this activity. Christians consider it an honor to be chosen for such ministry and are glad for an opportunity to work for the Lord. Often they go out two by two. They may walk a long distance once or twice a week to care for their outstation. There is no thought of financial remuneration—it is their service to the Lord.

Lay Preachers

Occasionally the lay worker will be given opportunity to report the progress of his outstation to the main church. Sometimes the congregation divides forces, sending a small group to accompany each local worker to his respective outstation to contribute with song and testimony to the success of the service. Often it is possible to establish Sunday school classes in the outstation. Sometimes a revival breaks out in the outstation and the main church will feel the throb of new life as the new converts come in to fill the ranks. Thus the whole assembly shares in the spreading of the gospel. The pastor visits these stations as he is able, but often the local workers carry on without help for weeks at a time.

As groups of converts form in these outstations, they receive instruction in Christian doctrine and conduct, in preparation for baptism. Presently, another group is ready to be organized into a church. The pastor of the main church then talks the matter over with them, consulting with the presbyter of the district also. If it is agreed that the time is ripe for organizing the church, the group quite likely will ask the lay worker who has been instrumental in raising up the work to come to them as their pastor. They agree to bring him food and to pay their tithes.

Perhaps this lay worker has in the meantime felt the hand of God upon his life leading him into a fuller ministry, and so is prepared to accept the call. Thus it often works out that we not only have a new church, but also a new worker. He in turn will begin to send out his converts into the surrounding territory, and the process begins all over again with the message of life reaching an ever-widening area.

A New Church Is Born

When the time comes for the short-term Bible school to open, there is no necessity of urging such young workers to attend. They have preached all they know, sometimes using the same message again and again. They are anxious to learn more. Problems have arisen which they have been unable to solve. So when Bible school opens, they will be there.

If his church is not too far away, the worker will likely continue caring for it on weekends, returning to the school each Monday to continue his studies. If it is far removed, the deacons will have to carry on for him, with the help of neighboring pastors, during the four-month term. As for the new worker, we can be sure that he will not be an indifferent student. It is a real joy to minister to such men, giving to them the much needed teaching they so earnestly desire.

As a result of such activities in one section of El Salvador, there is an established church every eight or ten miles in almost every direction. Within a radius of some 20 miles there are at least 25 self-supporting churches, each with its own pastor. Since each of these assemblies has from three to twelve lay preachers who are caring for outstations with new groups of believers constantly being formed, the work continues to expand.°

One such church, called Filadelfia, is located about 8 miles from Santa Ana. It has a membership of less than 100. It would be larger but time after time it has given up a portion of its members to form the nucleus of a new church. This church has used about 10 lay workers continually during the past number of years. These men carry the gospel week by week into the surrounding area. As they develop their ministry, many of them become full-time workers. A count was made a few years ago, and we found that there were then 26 full-time workers serving as pastors and evangelists who had been converted and trained in practical Christian work by that one assembly. All this has been done without the presence of a missionary.

This remarkable work is the product of the labors of a staunch national convert. He had little gift as a preacher, but he had a clear vision of the work of the church, and of the necessity of teaching his converts. He also had a remarkable capacity for pushing his converts into active service. He so established this church, and taught the converts, that they themselves now know how to establish a group of converts and

---

*Present strength (1983) of the Assemblies of God in El Salvador: organized churches, 780; ordained and licensed ministers, 800; outstations, 2,350; lay workers, 3,319; baptized members, 80,000; adherents, 100,000; baptized in the Holy Spirit, 40,000. All officials of the national organization are El Salvadoreans. There are four resident missionary couples and one schoolteacher. Nationals are being prepared as teachers for the Bible school. Seven of the national officers and zone presbyters are supported by the pastors and churches.

form them into a local church without the aid of a missionary or national official. Some of the outstanding pastors and officials in El Salvador are a product of this church. The pastor who founded the church went to be with Christ a few years ago, but the church has maintained its vigorous program under successive pastors. This assembly demonstrates the possibilities of self-propagation.

Now that we have observed the important role which the local churches play in the evangelization of a district where there is already a small beginning, let us examine the process by which a missionary may bring such a group of self-propagating churches into existence in a new district.

The Missionary as Evangelist

In pioneering a new area, the missionary exercises his first and most important ministry as a planter of churches. Here the missionary must be evangelist to the unconverted and teacher to the newborn converts. Instead of settling down to pastor the first group of converts that he raises up, the missionary should remain mobile and keep the vision for the entire district. . . . He should become a sort of circuit rider, visiting the towns and villages in the district when favorable circumstances give him an opening. He should always give particular attention to those points where the Spirit of God seems to be moving in a special way, but refuse to stay in one place so long that the people come to depend upon him as their pastor.

When the missionary makes his monthly or bi-monthly tour of the field, he will do well to encourage national brethren, who give promise of usefulness for God, to accompany him. Should he already have the help of a national worker with some experience in gospel work who has come, perhaps, from a neighboring district, so much the better; but if not, let the missionary keep on the lookout for promising "Timothys" among the converts, inviting such to accompany him on his tours. Care should be taken from

Take Promising Converts Along

the first, however, that the missionary does not foster in the young worker a spirit of financial dependence upon himself by offering him financial remuneration or by assuming an undue portion of the travel expenses. The tour should be a partnership in the work of the gospel.

This companionship on the missionary trail has a fourfold purpose. *First,* it enables the missionary to inspire and instruct the young workers more effectively than he would be able to do in a classroom. *Second,* the need of the field and the opportunities for gospel work in the district, viewed with the missionary, are impressed upon the young worker, thus inspiring his evangelistic fervor and preparing him to answer God's call to meet the need which he has seen. *Third,* the new groups of believers become accustomed to the ministry of a national, rather than that of the missionary, so that when the moment comes for them to establish themselves as a local congregation, they will doubtless ask some such worker to come to them as their pastor. *Last,* the presence of nationals with the missionary inspires confidence in the hearers.

This intimate association helps the missionary to interpret correctly the attitudes, customs and problems which he finds. Thus he himself is educated in national ways and avoids what otherwise might be serious blunders in dealing with the people.

As groups of converts come into existence, the missionary will assume his second role: that of teacher. He will give instruction in Christian doctrine and conduct. He will also encourage them in the task of propagating the gospel, showing them how to go about the establishing of churches and outstations. He will organize the groups in the manner explained in the preceding chapter. He will then leave them in charge of their own national leaders, with only an occasional visit from himself to guide and inspire them.

Of increasing importance in today's world is the evangelizing of the large cities. All over the world people are migrating from rural areas to the large centers of population. Searching for a better life and more opportunities for their children, they come by the thousands to the industrial centers of the country. In Latin America it is not uncommon to find one-fifth to one-third of the population in the capital city.

Evangelizing the Large Cities

This presents to the Church both a tremendous opportunity and a heavy responsibility. Probably there is no time when an individual is more open to receive the gospel than at the particular period when he has left his friends and relatives of his home town and finds himself in a completely new environment. He may now feel free to accept the gospel when perhaps previously social ties may have hindered him. At any rate, we have found that our churches multiply rapidly as they minister the gospel to these "displaced" persons.

However, there is a more fundamental reason why the cities are of importance. The life of the nation is principally directed from the cities. It is in the cities where the schools, universities, government installations, etc., are established. To fail to reach the city with the gospel is to fail to evangelize the country.

The method mentioned previously of extension of the church by establishing outstations through the ministry of lay workers is valid for the cities as well as rural areas. Experience has shown that the mother-church method of establishing daughter churches can be eminently successful with proper team work, teaching, and inspiration.

It has been often noted that it is difficult for rural ministers to come into the city and pastor city churches. The establishing of a network of churches in the city requires that there be workers available from the city itself. This presents a problem inasmuch as the men most qualified to lead city churches are those men who themselves live in the city, but who usually find themselves hindered from attending a Bible school because of family responsibilities. We believe that at least a partial answer to this is the establishing of a night Bible school for the training of lay workers who eventually can develop into pastors. This program is being carried on with success in many of the large cities of Latin America and is providing the opportunity of training many workers who otherwise would have remained in the role of a church member. A worker so trained can carry on the work of an outstation even while he is studying; and once he is through with his course of studies, he can give more attention to his outstation. Eventually the outstation could develop into a church; and as the church grows in strength, the pastor can leave his secular employment and devote his entire time to the work of the ministry. Once this step is taken, it is not difficult to envision that he may later transfer to another city and assume pastoral responsibilities there.

Salvation-Healing Campaigns

Some evangelists, both nationals and missionaries, have had a very successful ministry in establishing churches in the cities by means of salvation-healing campaigns. There have been abuses in this area because of certain evangelists who have made exaggerated claims or who have seemed to be more interested in the large crowds rather than in establishing the church. This has brought a certain amount of disrepute to the whole concept of emphasizing physical healing in relation to gospel campaigns. Even so, we must recall that Jesus himself used the healing of the sick as a means of ministering to people's spiritual as well as physical needs. Also, healing formed a prominent part in the apostles' ministry. We can only overlook this, then, to our own hurt. If the evangelist will keep this aspect of his campaigns in proper balance and remain humble, God can use this emphasis as a powerful means of attracting people to the gospel. Large cities throughout Latin America have received a tremendous impact for the gospel in this way, and dozens of good churches have been established. In order to achieve the best results from a salvation-healing campaign, a few guidelines should be observed:

1. There should be some planning toward the establishing of a permanent church. There is not much value in an evangelist stirring up interest in thousands of people and winning dozens or perhaps hundreds of converts and then leaving them without anyone to care for them. So, if a campaign is to be held in a new area, plans must be made from the beginning for a pastor to shepherd the flock. Also, as the meeting progresses it is necessary to think about a permanent location so that the meeting can go on after the evangelist leaves.

2. In a new area the evangelist should plan for a protracted meeting. Three to six months, preaching every night, is none too long to win the converts and prepare them to take their part in the life of the local church. Then the new converts should be taught while the meeting is still in progress. If the evangelist has a co-worker who is planning to stay on as pastor, the co-worker is the logical one to give daily instructions to the new converts, preparing them for baptism. The "Standard of Doctrine and Practice," which is included as an appendix of this book, will serve as an excellent guide for the worker to give necessary teaching to the new converts.

3. If a meeting has been particularly successful, rather than establishing one church, sometimes a half dozen or more churches can be founded. This depends, of course, on local conditions and availability of workers who can become pastors of these new efforts. After a campaign of several weeks in San Salvador, 350 new converts were instructed and baptized in water. The number of interested people, of course, included

several hundred others. These converts were divided into twelve groups in twelve different sections of the city with the result that at the end of one year's time there were twelve churches established with a total attendance of 1,500 in Sunday school. At the present time the work has grown in this city until there are forty churches. The Assemblies of God in Guatemala City experienced a similar expansion after a successful campaign, and ten churches were started in that city in one year's time. God is still using His mighty works to win people to salvation in His Son, Jesus.

RETHINK THIS CHAPTER

1. What is the key to evangelizing a mission field?
2. How may missionaries unwittingly discourage the national converts' zeal to witness?
3. Explain the system of developing outstations used in Central America.
4. How does the employment of this system result in new churches and new workers? Illustrate.
5. How may a missionary begin to evangelize a new district?
6. What benefits are derived when the missionary takes promising workers with him on his itinerary?
7. Explain the importance of urban evangelism.
8. Give some guidelines for evangelistic campaigns in large cities.

5

Developing Leadership

The government and extension of the church in any land must eventually be left in the hands of national leaders. These men are Christ's own gift to His church (Ephesians 4:11-13). Without such men, the task of establishing an indigenous church would be hopeless. Since it is precisely at this point that many missions have failed, we shall endeavor to point out some of the mistakes of the past, giving also some constructive suggestions.

Let us again bring our objective into clear focus. Our aim is to develop the national church rather than the mission station. We are to provide leadership for the national church, not merely helpers for the missionary. Missionaries often unconsciously reflect a wrong concept when they talk about "my helper" or "my worker." The national pastor or evangelist is Christ's gift to His church, not to the missionary. Let us begin by asking some questions:

Our objectives should include the following: **What Do We Want?**

First, our workers training program should aim at developing spiritual, soul-winning churches.

Second, the immediate objective should be the preparation of lay workers and full-time workers to man an expanding program of evangelism and care for the new churches that thus will be raised up.

Third, the long-range program calls for the preparation of spiritual leaders in all spheres of ministry so that they will be able to carry on a fully developed, indigenous church program.

**Are We
Reaching Our
Objectives?**

While we rejoice in the evidence of very good results which we have seen, and praise God for the consecrated effort of every missionary, as well as the dedication of the national workers, there is probably not one among us who is completely satisfied. The most optimistic among us would admit that we are only partially reaching these objectives. Here are some of the less flattering facts which we must face.

First, many of the churches raised up are not truly soul-winning agencies of the kingdom of God. Those that are reasonably active and successful are usually not functioning to the maximum of their potential, while others are almost entirely unproductive in this respect.

Second, many of the pastors and workers produced by mission schools have not turned out to be real soul winners nor have manifested true spiritual leadership. While there are notable exceptions, many times workers lack initiative and depend too much on the mission for guidance and financial support. This is not intended to be an indictment of either the missionary or the worker.

Something has been missing, and neither the missionary nor the worker may know what it is! It is not necessarily lack of consecration, nor lack of love to God, although few of us would claim that our spiritual life could not be improved in this regard!

Third, some workers seem to feel that after they have been to school they are above pioneering a church or working in rural areas. Perhaps this is a reflection of the general modern movement toward the large cities. However, we cannot doubt that there is a measure of failure in our training program if the men we are training are unwilling to return to the churches and the areas with which they are familiar and which present a great spiritual challenge. In this case, we are at least partially training them *away* from the task instead of *for* the task.

It may be that there are gaps in our training program.

Where Have We Failed?

First, there may be a gap between the intellectual development and the spiritual development of the worker. Too often we have trained the mind and have not been able to lead the student into the full life in the Holy Spirit.

Second, there may be a gap between knowledge and practical ministry. We place a student in school and nurture him in a somewhat artificial climate. He is often too far removed for too long a period of time from the rugged life and problems which he is to meet in the ministry.

Third, we may have left too wide a gap between the clergy and laity. Our training program should aim to put the entire church on the march for God.

Fourth, there may be a serious gap in our concept of the role that the training of workers plays in the development of the church. Some train only to fill vacancies. A Latin American minister in a kindly way voiced his criticism of our workers' training program, saying that we were training too many prospective workers. He said his own denomination looked ahead and saw that in the future they would need six or seven more pastors. Then they trained that number and, when a class finished seminary work, there was a place assured for each one. There was no question of support nor what this worker would do. On the other hand, he said, "You train more workers than you have openings for, and then many must fill an inferior place or get along without support." My answer to that is that we are training workers for invasion. We do not expect merely to hold our own, but we expect to train far more workers than we have churches. We believe that this is the way that new churches will come into existence. A man trained under the other concept would not be expected to exercise personal initiative. Someone else would do the planning for him and finance his efforts. I fear that following such a concept would never permit us to evangelize the world in our generation.

Fifth, we may be neglecting to train the right men. It is important that the missionary shall not limit his leadership training to the bright young men who at first glance would appear to be the best material. This is one of the fundamental errors of modern missions. The missionary has failed to see the importance of making place for mature men—the "elders" of the New Testament. Instead, he has gathered around him a group of the brightest minds, usually boys from the mission school or children of converts, to give them special instruction. One missionary stated his policy in these words: "He [the missionary] lays hold of the best elements of the race [i.e., young boys of quick intelligence] to whom he ministers, training them into a force which he can use."

These boys are kept on the mission station at mission expense over a period of years. If they prove to be apt students, they become assistants to the foreign missionary, at times performing tasks at the station, at other times taking short evangelistic trips into the surrounding area to distribute literature or to hold gospel services. They may be given charge at outstations. Later they may be sent to a theological seminary, and afterward placed in charge of churches under the oversight of the missionary.

But often, just when the missionary begins to hope that he is accomplishing his task of providing a trained, national ministry for the church, he finds that deep-seated troubles exist; that in spite of all of their training, his national workers are inadequate. This inadequacy is sometimes intangible and difficult to analyze. One or more weaknesses may be present.

For one thing, the worker may not be able to *lead* the national church. Perhaps he preaches well but his fellow countrymen do not really accept him as their leader. They constantly appeal to the missionary over the head of the local pastor, or else they follow the advice of strong lay leaders in the congregation whose ideas are often opposed to those of the pastor.

Then, he may lack initiative. He waits for the missionary to tell him to visit a new locality. Even when he goes, he often is not able to make the most of the opportunities presented.

Again, he may experience difficulty in adjusting himself to the humble surroundings of the community to which he ministers, feeling that to adapt himself to the lowly customs of the villagers would be a step down for him.

Also, he may continue to depend on the missionary to meet his financial needs and be unable to demonstrate a robust faith in God.

In such circumstances, a missionary may become discouraged with the worker and decide that it was a mistake to have trained him. He may even despair of ever being able to train national converts for successful leadership. Before he reaches such an unhappy conclusion, the missionary would do well to reflect that such national workers are not entirely to blame for their inadequacy. Let us observe the causes that have produced these deficiencies.

The worker's training from boyhood has largely been under semiforeign influence and under circumstances which have separated him from his national environment.

Causes of Inadequacies

Furthermore, he has been trained in Western learning rather than in the wisdom of his race. Consequently, he seems to his own people to be half foreign. They do not easily accept him as their leader because his ways are different, and in some cases, even his style of speech has been affected.

It is true that he lacks initiative. Has he not all his life been subject to the rule of the missionary? He has always been corrected and sometimes punished when he failed to do as the missionary desired. If he displeases the missionary now, the missionary has power to remove him from his position and church. His only safety lies in obeying the missionary and in making sure that he doesn't displease him. Is it any wonder that he lacks initiative?

Granted that he looks too much to the missionary for his support. What else could be expected? Has not the missionary always provided for him, first in school, then in his outstation work, afterward in the seminary and finally in his pastorate? The training of his whole life has been one of dependence upon the missionary. It is too much to expect that a lifetime of training can be overcome just because he has now become a pastor of a church. This is especially true when the missionary still handles the funds and allots the salaries.

What Must We Do?   We must seek the New Testament approach and follow the New Testament pattern. I have the deep conviction that every deficiency in our work can be traced to a failure to follow the New Testament pattern. True indigenous church principles are in reality New Testament church principles. We might be shocked if we could bring ourselves face to face with the discrepancies between our methods and the New Testament pattern. We may be completely orthodox in our *theology* and be a long way from the New Testament example in our *practice*. How easy it is to accept the established pattern as the right pattern! We think it is right because our predecessors followed this way or it is the pattern established by other missions. Yet experience is teaching us that the established modern pattern of missions is not sufficient to meet the demands of the day. We will never reach the world for Christ in our generation if we simply follow in the groove worn for us by our predecessors. The New Testament approach is a *flexible* approach. It leaves room for the guidance of the Holy Spirit. Not all situations are to be met in the same way. This brings up a very serious question. Are we spiritual leaders of a sufficient stature to be able to determine the mind of God for the problems of our particular field, or will we insist on following through on a predetermined course? I would like to break this down into a few practical suggestions.

First, we must provide for the spiritual development of our prospective workers as well as their intellectual development. Jesus chose the disciples first of all that they might "be with Him" and after that that they should preach and heal the sick. Many times He called His disciples apart for spiritual instruction. He took them with Him in the ministry and, as far as they were able to follow, through Gethsemane and Calvary. In a very real sense, they went with Him through the resurrection. Even so, He required that they spend ten days waiting in Jerusalem for the fullness of the Spirit before they were to go "into all the world." Too often in modern practice we have neglected this phase of training. We train in theology, homiletics and church history, but how seldom do our students learn the deeper meanings of the cross, the resurrection and the indwelling Spirit!

Second, we must integrate our training program with the national church. Its pace should be synchronized with the tempo of the national church, and its program should be such that it will truly meet the needs of the church. There is a tendency for institutions to become an end in themselves instead of a means to an end. Sometimes missionaries feel that the Bible school is their particular sphere of influence, and they carry on quite independently of the national church. However, it is the national church that is to furnish the students, and it is the national church that is to be served. The church should feel that the training program is their own and that the trained workers produced are their own workers, not the mission's.

Third, the workers should be trained to the task, not away from it! Some institutions seem to have for an objective the sealing off of the student from his ordinary life. The directors seem to feel that it is necessary to separate the student and infuse in him the school spirit and build his character under the direct supervision of the school in order that he may be properly prepared for the work which he is to do. Probably there are some advantages, but it is difficult to know how a student who is kept in an artificial climate of a theological school for three years or more can make the proper adjustment to the demands of rugged pioneer work when his schooling is finished. The New Testament approach is more along the line of on-the-job training. Jesus taught His disciples, but He took them with Him. When He said, "Look on the fields; the harvest truly is great," He was in the midst of visible need. The harvest field was not something found on a missionary map of the world, but was rather portrayed in the needs of the sick and sinful that were surrounding them on every side. Jesus taught His disciples, and then sent them out to preach and to heal the sick. When they were confronted with failures, as in the case of the man with a lunatic son, He gave further instruction. He taught them on the job. In Acts 19 Paul had a training school in Ephesus where he taught for two full years. Lest anyone think this was classroom instruction only, read the following statement that "so all Asia heard the Word of the Lord." Certainly Paul himself did not take this message personally to all Asia. He taught, and with on-the-job training, the workers and elders that were raised up under his ministry were the messengers that accomplished this tremendous task of evangelism.

Fourth, we must provide for the training of the entire church rather than the exclusive training of a select few who will be devoting themselves to full-time ministry. We must in our training fill in the artificial gap that seems to exist between clergy and laity. The whole church functions as the body of Christ with every individual Christian having his place and his ministry. Certainly all are not called to be preachers or teachers, but all are called to work for God. The whole church is a functioning organism. How far we have drifted from this in our churches in America and, therefore, how difficult it is for us to inaugurate a New Testament pattern on the foreign field! We tend to give training only to some who will become ministers, thus sadly neglecting the entire body of Christ, the army of witnesses that God intends to bring the gospel to every creature. Can we let such immense manpower go to waste and still expect to succeed in our task?

Jesus not only sent out the twelve but "other seventy also." What place do we have for the "other seventy also" in our present training program? The New Testament church had not only apostles but, when these stayed in Jerusalem after the persecution which came at the death of Stephen, the *disciples* were scattered abroad and went everywhere preaching the Word. I believe that we are missing a tremendous opportunity for the Kingdom by failing to develop a lay ministry. Ordinarily training programs are set up in such a way that only the younger people can attend. Those who have family responsibilities find no way to meet these responsibilities and get the necessary training. Often, too, insufficient provision is made for those who do not have the necessary schooling to prepare them to carry the heavier studies. I believe that the church has the obligation to provide training for everyone that God is calling. It does not have to be the same degree of training for all; rather, teaching should be tailored to fit the need of each class. Remember too that the worker is not required to have all of the knowledge available before he begins to work. It is necessary for the one that teaches to be only one step ahead of those who are taught. The new convert can witness to the unsaved, and older converts can help the new converts. The pastor can help the deacons and local workers; the missionaries and Bible school instructors can help the pastors. Converts can become Sunday school teachers; Sunday school teachers can become lay workers; lay workers can become pastors. If all birds refused to sing because they could not equal the nightingale, the forest would be a silent place.

When a farmer is harvesting a fruit crop, he not only needs a truck with a driver, but also for each truck he needs several men with baskets who will handpick the fruit and bring it to the truck. There is no advantage in multiplying the number of trucks and truck drivers above the amount of pickers who will in turn fill the trucks. This is a rather crude illustration of the importance of the lay preacher. We have concentrated on the training of the "driver"; we need to give more attention to getting more "pickers" out on the field.

Fifth, we must not neglect the older converts. In New Testament times, the church laid hold of the more mature elements among the converts and these became the church elders. Some had ministry in the Word and others helped govern the work. Let us see what we can find in favor of this arrangement.

Can we really improve on the model given us in the New Testament? Do we not subject the work to grave dangers and weaknesses when we substitute a system of our own (even though time-honored and widely followed) for the New Testament method?

These men are recognized as men of mature judgment by their own people and are their natural leaders. Thus there is no question of leadership being thrust upon the local congregation by a foreign missionary.

These elders know their own people and are schooled in the wisdom of their own race. It is true that they will carry on things in their own way rather than in the American way, but is not this necessary if the church is to be truly indigenous?

The growth of the Christian ministry of such an elder will be natural rather than forced. The people of the community will think of him as one of their own number, rather than as a professional Christian employee of a foreign mission. His influence will be proportionately greater. The elder will grow into the ministry as a result of normal Christian development, and his growth will not be a "hothouse" growth fostered in a mission station. His zeal to work for God will be the result of his spiritual experience. His desire will be to make Christ known and he will be happy for an opportunity to preach in outstations and surrounding villages. When he is given Bible training, it will be because he *is* a gospel worker; not in the hope that training will make him one.

He will be already established in business or farming; therefore the missionary will not have to support him. The day should come when the local church will assume his support in order to free him for full-time service, but he will always be largely free from the fault, so common to mission-trained workers, of looking to the missionary for the supply of his financial needs.

These elders introduce a mature element in the administration of church affairs. They represent a national Christian leadership, thus providing a stabilizing influence in the government of the church. Moreover, their decisions will be formed from the national point of view—an indispensable factor in the building of a strong national church. This factor is entirely lacking when missionaries make the decisions which in turn must be accepted without question by mission-trained workers.

In Nicaragua a man was converted at the age of 58. Desirous of serving God, he entered Bible school at the age of 60. After his studies there, he served a Nicaraguan church as pastor for 15 years. We must not overlook men like him. If we train only young men because we can mold them and give them a complete theological education, we shall retard the development of the national church.

J. Herbert Kane comments,

"All things being equal, a man with a college education is better than one without. Naturally we missionaries would like to see some seminary men join the work in North Anhwei; but experience has taught us that these people do not always turn out well. They invariably have difficulty in adjusting themselves to the primitive conditions existing in the interior. Having once become accustomed to a semiwestern style of living in Shanghai or Hong Kong, they are unable, many of them, to "eat bitterness" along with the uncouth people of the country districts. Sooner or later they fall sick, or grow weary in well-doing, and drift to the larger cities, which offer more scope for their talents and better opportunity for advancement. Local men with a moderate amount of schooling have no such trouble. Having been brought up in the district they are part of the community. They are familiar with local customs; they speak the local dialect; and they eat the local food. Moreover, their shops and homes are there. Their farms and families are there.

This gives stability to the work, and stability always makes for permanency."[1]

It may be objected that elders with so little training cannot be trusted to do things in the proper way. Yet, the apostle Paul trusted them. It is doubtless true that they will make mistakes, but the missionary himself makes mistakes even after years of service. Probably the real objection is that the missionary feels that this type of worker introduces an element into the work over which he has very little control. But is this a bad thing? We cannot have missionary-dominated workers and a strong national church at the same time. Paul commended the elders and the churches "to the Holy Ghost." Cannot we trust the same Holy Spirit to give true leadership to the local churches through their own elders? May God increase our faith!

Of course, some very real problems present themselves in training these more mature men for leadership. Young men can leave their homes for extended periods of time to receive Bible training, while the older men are tied down with family and business obligations. At least some of the difficulty arises from the fact that missionaries are given to patterning a program after the Bible institute or seminary in the homeland, instead of adapting it to the needs of the field. Sometimes, too, natural love of institutions causes the missionary to permit the institution to become an end in itself. He is actually striving to make the Bible school a great institution instead of merely using it as a tool for attaining a greater end: the development of the national church. If our present methods are not helping us to reach our goal of a strong indigenous church, then those methods should be revised or discarded.

Adapt Bible Training to the field

Accessibility of the Bible school is a point of importance. Within certain limits, we should put access-

[1] J. Herbert Kane, *Twofold Growth*, pp. 156-57.

sibility to the student first and convenience to the missionary second. Of course, such matters as climate and health, both for the student and missionary, must influence the decision as to locality. In an agricultural community, seedtime and harvest must also be taken into account so the farm workers may be able to attend. Most of the people are very poor and, since we do not intend to assume their support, we should not inaugurate a program that would deprive them of their only opportunity of making a living. In a city it may be necessary to limit the training program to night classes. We should be versatile enough to meet the demands of changing circumstances.

Advantages of Short School Terms

Then the *length of the course* must be considered. In Central America we have found that if we are to keep the mature men coming to Bible training school, four months is about as long as we can hold one course. Some have urged upon us the regular eight- or nine-month term, but we found if we did this that our older men with families could not come.

Mature students will have to make some provision for their families. Some of them are pastors of small churches. If they do not come from too great a distance, they can return to care for their families and churches over weekends. But if the term is too long, they are unable to bear the financial strain. And the worker is unable to care for his church. For that reason we have kept the school term short.

Another advantage of a short training course is that there is less danger of overloading the student with knowledge beyond his spiritual capacity. Training should keep pace with spiritual development. When knowledge exceeds spiritual growth, we develop a superficial worker—a man long on theory and ability but short on experience in Christian living. It is better to give a man four months of study and eight months to work out in his life and ministry the knowledge gained, than to give him eight or nine months of study at one time with only a short vacation before beginning another term. The student does not have sufficient opportunity to absorb the knowledge already received and put theory into practice. After finishing one course of four months' study, students often skip a year. This is a distinct advantage, for when the worker does come back to school he has much greater capacity to receive new instruction. Consequently he gets much more help from the course than if he had attended without interruption.

There is a real advantage in having a *decentralized training program.* The school can then be carried to the districts and it is not necessary to depend entirely upon students coming to the central location. The nearer we can keep our training program to the source of workers (the local churches), the more effective it will be. Perhaps there is no better method for strengthening the churches of a district than to take a short course of Bible studies to one of the central churches of the area. These short annual courses may be from one week to one month in duration. Deacons, lay workers and Sunday school teachers, together with other Christians desirous of engaging in Christian service, gather from nearby churches for classes every day during this period.

Decentralized Training Program

Food is contributed by offerings from the churches and perhaps a small quota is paid by each student. Thus we can give the students training right in the very locality in which they are to work.

Those attending this short course have their appetite whetted for a more complete course of studies in the regular Bible school. If practical evangelism is carried on at the same time, the short course serves as a stimulus to all the churches in the area.

The training program should be adapted to each field. In some areas a night school rather than the regular day boarding school has proved to be most effective. This is particularly valid in the large cities where many of the students will be working during the day and have no opportunity to attend the day Bible school.

Sometimes the day Bible school offers night classes for those who cannot attend in the day time. Again, there are occasions when a school will also offer studies in another city. This usually takes the form of night classes. Sometimes the studies are limited to the first year courses. It does give an opportunity, however, to raise up an army of layworkers and prospective pastors from an area not readily accessible to the central school.

The concept of theological education by extension has born fruit in recent years. Under this plan members of the faculty of the Bible school travel to determined sections of the country where small groups of students meet once every week or two. The students are given assignments to be reported on at the following meeting. The result has been that many who could not come to a central school have been able to receive ministerial training. This type of effort can be very difficult and time consuming for the professor. It also requires specially prepared lessons to enable the student to study on his own. However, the results have been gratifying and the increased number of students prepared as layworkers, or pastors, makes the extra effort well worthwhile.

The *course of studies* given in the Bible school should be arranged to meet the needs of the field, taking into account local problems, customs and the religious views of the community. It is usually not sufficient merely to duplicate or translate Bible study courses from Bible schools in the homeland. Often these courses must be simplified or revised in order that the students may receive maximum benefit.

It is well for the missionary who plans to teach in

a Bible school to get practical experience in the country by close contact with the people in their everyday life. He should acquire firsthand knowledge of the problems peculiar to the area before he undertakes a teaching ministry. If, on the other hand, he endeavors to give advice on problems when he is still unfamiliar with the background, he is almost certain to make serious blunders. An intimate knowledge of the people is a prerequisite for the training of workers.

Train by Association

Let the missionary remember that his personal association with the workers is a most important factor in their training. Jesus took disciples with Him. Let the missionary travel with his workers on foot, on horseback, by truck, train, or bus as the opportunity affords. Let him eat with them at the same table and at night share the same room. Questions of all categories will be brought up—doctrinal, social, and personal. The worker will learn much from the missionary's words, but more from his attitudes. Through such contacts the missionary gains opportunities of imparting not only his knowledge but also his own spirit and vision.

The goal is to develop not only pastors for local congregations, but leaders also for every ministry that the church will need. Evangelistic, teaching, and executive abilities must be developed. God gives the gift of government, the word of knowledge, and the word of wisdom to various men among the converts. The church must have the men, and the missionary needs vision to detect and select them from among the converts, and patience to develop them so that they can fulfill their calling.

Train for Teaching and Executive Positions

The Bible school and the churches need teachers, so the missionary must thrust the responsibility of teaching upon men who have a budding gift along that line. The church needs national executives to help solve difficult problems and provide adequate leadership for advancement. Again the missionary must thrust the responsibility for decision upon these men—withdrawing himself from the scene—and leave the responsibility upon their shoulders for increasingly long periods of time. Everyone learns by doing. There is no other way of developing teachers and leaders than for the missionary to prepare men as best as he can by teaching, and then put them to work, even though they are not yet fully capable of performing the task. If we insist that men must be fully capable before we trust them with responsibility, we shall never be ready to let go of the reins of government.

Free and Open Discussion

In the development of leadership, whether pastors or officials who will hold a position in the national organization, it is important that both missionaries and nationals understand the value of free and open discussion in arriving at decisions and solving problems. We have all seen good men in a position of leadership who, because they have failed to consult with their associates, have been a disappointment to their fellow workers. Their administration failed for lack of coordination and cooperation.

"In an indigenous work the brethren need not only Bible teaching, they also must learn how to deal with the administrative and other problems which are essentially bound up with the life of the church . . . for the missionary to decide these matters for them either by imposing his fiat or by the subtler method of discussions to approve his wish, is to hinder the development of the native brethren. They need to be awakened to the nature of the problem so that they may appreciate the solution and perceive how to apply it to their own varying conditions, and this awakening comes only through one and another discussing the matter from his viewpoint and circumstances. . . . The democratic method of free decision after full discussion is not infallible, but neither is the dictatorial fiat. On the other hand, it has the very great merits of decision by the natives, who know their people and customs; of readier acceptance and support; of correction if mistaken; and, above all, of educating the constituency in the matters of government. Without this there cannot be a truly indigenous church."[2]

Some missionaries have shown a reluctance to place themselves on common ground with the nationals in meeting a problem. They have felt that to ask advice is to lower their position in the eyes of the workers. This is a mistaken attitude, not only because the missionary thus deprives himself of the valuable contribution that the nationals can make to him in correctly interpreting their own people and problems, but also because he misses an excellent opportunity to instruct the workers by his own example in the process of solving problems by group discussion and group decision.

The missionary should refrain from using the opportunity for discussion to gain his own end by the weight of his argument or by the force of his personality, so that his plan is accepted even when no true agreement has been reached. He must wait for the slower minds to think things through, and *never assume that silence gives consent.* Sometimes even "yes" really means "no," and when the missionary takes a hesitant "yes" to mean that the brethren approve, he is quite likely to find the problem back again within a few days, as unsolved as ever. If we force upon the nationals a decision that is not really their own, they will get out from under the yoke which we have placed upon them at the first opportunity. When we are not there to enforce the decision, it will not be enforced because it was not really theirs. They merely said "yes" to please the missionary, but their heart was not in it.

Patience is required in such discussions. The mis-

[2]John Ritchie, *Indigenous Church Principles in Theory and Practice*, p. 56.

sionary should refrain from doing all the talking, and draw the brethren out little by little until he really understands their fears and the cause of their reluctance. Even when their remarks seem needlessly long and beside the point, he should allow them to take their verbal excursions. Presently they will make a statement or ask a question that will help him to get at the heart of the matter. Then, and only then, will he be able to guide the brethren to a decision that will truly meet their approval.

Sometimes he may not be able to convince them 100 percent of the correctness of his own opinion. But then, he may not be 100 percent right! Even though he were entirely right, yet it would be better to bring them along with him wholeheartedly half of the way and stop there temporarily, knowing that it had been their decision, than to insist on their going all the way against their own judgment. Later on he may hope to show them the advisability of taking further steps. For the moment, he has made strides toward his goal in that the nationals are making the decisions and in the right direction.

Avoid Bypassing National Leaders

Having placed men in positions of authority, or having allowed the church to do so, the missionary should be careful not to snatch up the reins of authority again and bypass the national leaders. Probably most missionaries have been guilty of this. As the *Indian Standard* says, "We complain of their lack of independence, and then outvote them whenever they show a spark of it." We teach that the church is to be self-governing, but when some important problem comes up, instead of presenting the matter for the decision of the national leaders, we simply tell them what to do. We disregard their position, set them to one side, and do as we think best. Then they know that although we talk about the nationals taking responsibility and assuming leadership, yet in reality we do not permit it. They know that when a decision of importance is to be made, we will do as we please. Thus they not only fail to follow us in our decisions, with a corresponding lack of coordination in the work, but resentments may develop and schisms form between nationals and missionaries.

As the missionary by precept and example teaches both the value of group discussion and group decision, he prepares the nationals for the time when the full responsibility shall be left in their own hands. Thus each one learns that he is not to decide important questions on his own individual responsibility, but that major decisions are reached and policies laid down after full and open discussion with his brethren. This will be a safeguard in administration and for the church as a whole.

RETHINK THIS CHAPTER

1. Name three objectives of the training program for national leaders.
2. Where may we be failing to reach our objectives?
3. What might be the causes for these weaknesses?
4. How might this situation be remedied?
5. In what sense may training be too narrowly based?
6. What place did *elders* hold in the New Testament church?
7. Show different ways that Bible school training may be adapted to the field.
8. Explain the importance of free and open discussion with church leaders.
9. How may missionaries bypass national leaders?

6

Self-support

Self-support is not necessarily the most important aspect of the indigenous church, but it is undoubtedly the most discussed. In fact, some speak as though a self-supporting church were identical with an indigenous church. We have already pointed out that this is not the case, for a congregation may be able to support itself and still not have initiative for evangelism or the ability to govern itself.

It is regrettable that the use of money by the missionary has often weakened the church rather than strengthened it. The right use of money has its place in the missionary program, but if missionaries were to be faced with the choice of too much money or too little, it would probably be better for the church if the missionaries chose too little. When the missionary does not have money, he must depend on God and encourage national initiative. There are self-supporting works in existence today, due not so much to the wisdom of the missionary, as to the fact that he had very limited financial resources and could not offer financial help to national workers. Later he realized that what he had supposed was a hindrance to the work, was in reality a boon. A vigorous national church had been established.

Missionaries who make appeals asking for money to support national workers, to erect church buildings, etc., should carefully weigh the long-range consequences and be sure that their procedure will truly strengthen the church, not weaken it. The future of the church should not be sacrificed for the sake of temporary advantage. Missionaries who plead for funds, asking for foreign help to do for the national church that which it should rightfully do for itself, should examine their position to see if they are on scriptural ground. Sometimes we get the impression that the missionary believes that the work of the Holy Spirit depends on the amount of money available. The Word of the Lord is not bound: it is we who are "straitened" in our own vision and understanding.

Dangers in Use of Funds

E. Gideon, M.A. (Oxon) writes: "I have kept to the last what seems to me the most serious indictment of the work of the church. Most of the churches in India are not self-supporting. This is a very serious matter. Analyzed critically, it means this: Indian Christians take their religion so lightly and superficially that they are not prepared to contribute adequately to the support of their own churches and their own ministers. I do not know of any community outside India which would permit of such a state of affairs. And Missions and missionaries acquiesce in this, nay, encourage it by soliciting more and more money from abroad. But it seems to me that so long as Indians are not prepared to sacrifice whatever is necessary to support their churches, this is convincing proof that the church has failed in its fundamental objective—to convince a people of the truth of Christianity, for surely it is true in this, as in all ages of all peoples in all countries, that the only real test of conviction is the desire and willingness to sacrifice.

"It is a shameful thing that we cannot stand comparison in this matter with our Hindu and Muslim brethren. I think we have a right to ask the Missions why they have allowed things to come to such a pass, why they have so pauperized and weakened us that the indigenous church instead of being a sturdy, virile, self-reliant body, able and willing to be self-sufficient, is a feeble, weedy, topheavy administration, the members of which are always turning to the West with imploring eyes, and abject, outstretched hands asking for alms. In this, I maintain the church has failed in its most important work, and the measure of its material success in obtaining foreign men and foreign money is the exact measure of its spiritual failure in this country."

At a gathering of the Evangelical Foreign Missions Association, Rev. Soltau of Korea made this statement: "I am convinced that the amount of foreign feeling can nearly always be expected in exact proportion to the amount of foreign funds used. The more foreign funds used in the work, the more anti-foreign sentiment you are likely to have." Another missionary has stated, "Practically all of the difficulties that have arisen on our field between missionaries and native workers can be traced back to money."

There is no doubt that the use of money by the missionary has been the cause of much resentment on the part of the nationals. The nationals do not understand the missionary's point of view; they think that he is not as generous as he should be, or that he is partial in his treatment of the workers. They may feel that the missionary uses the power which the distribution of funds places in his hands as a lever to get his own way. It is hard to get around the idea that the man who holds the purse strings is the boss. The real mistake in all this has been in teaching the converts to look to the missionary as a source of income.

The church on the mission field should be self-supporting for the following reasons:

Reasons for Self-Support

First, it is the Bible plan. If this were the only reason for insisting on self-support, it would be sufficient. A reading of the Acts of the Apostles will convince anyone that this was the apostolic method.

We find no hint that the churches among the Gentiles were supported by the Jewish congregation. Instead we do find that the Apostle Paul solicited offerings from the churches he had founded to help relieve the distress among the famine-stricken saints in Jerusalem (Acts 24:17; Rom. 15:26). A striking contrast to today's procedure!

We accept tithing as a scriptural basis for the support of the work in the homeland. We believe that they who preach the gospel should live off the gospel. Circumstances may differ but the principle is the same everywhere. Why not apply it the world around?

Tithing Is the Bible Method

Second, it is a logical plan. Under ordinary circumstances even the poorest can support a pastor according to their own standard of living if there are ten or more faithful tithing families in the congregation. Some missionaries object on the ground that the people are too poor to support their pastor. They overlook the fact that these same people once supported their priests or witchdoctors in heathendom. Strangely enough, one missionary contended that the converts on his field were *too well off* to support their pastor! I had pointed out that the Christians on a certain field were very poor, the daily wage a mere pittance, yet they supported their own pastors. He informed me that this was possible because the people in the area were accustomed to poverty. "But our people are different," he reasoned, "they come from a higher class and we could not expect a pastor to live on what the people would give him."

Of course, if we introduce an American standard of living, it will require the equivalent of an American income to support the work. If we consider the preaching of the gospel as a profession, then it is logical that the pastor must live as a doctor or lawyer; and his support would be beyond the reach of a poor congregation. But if we follow the New Testament pattern, in which the pastor is one with his flock, and lives on the same level as the members of his congregation, then there is no reason why ten families who support themselves, cannot also support a pastor with their tithes.

Third, the spiritual welfare of the congregation demands that it be self-supporting. A sense of responsibility fosters spiritual blessings. Deprive the converts of the privilege of giving and the responsibility of sacrificing to support the work and weak Christians will result. They will likely be inactive also in evangelism and fail to assume the responsibility of church discipline. They will be willing to allow the missionary to do everything. On the other hand, they cherish a work which has cost them sacrifice and effort.

Take church property as an illustration. In a certain city, the Mission had furnished everything that the congregation needed when the work began. Land, building and benches were all provided. The congregation had the use of this property for more than twenty years.

I once visited there during a period when there was no resident missionary in the district. The congregation called my attention to the state of the building. They desired help for even the simplest repairs. We might ask: "Well, brethren, since you have had the use of this building for twenty years, isn't it time that you assume the cost of these repairs?" But they do not see it that way. The property belongs to the Mission, and one does not repair other people's property.

In the same country a new work was started. After a few months it became imperative to secure a property where the little group of converts could meet. We got together the funds that were available and the pastor secured a small loan; but it still was not enough. As we studied the situation, one of the brethren said, "I think that I can give so much more for this need." Another said, "I, too, will give the same amount," Seeing that they were doing their best, I made a personal offering also. The property was secured and the pastor and his little congregation went to work. They repaired the building inside and out. They laid a cement floor to take the place of the dirt one. After a few months it was a much better building than when it was purchased. The sense of responsibility and ownership made the difference.

Some of our congregations in Central America have struggled for ten years to build their chapel. They have begun in a private home, moved into a thatch-roofed hut of their own, and finally after years of sacrifice and labor, have completed their frame or adobe building. Their little chapel means infinitely more to them than if it had been provided by the Mission.

Congregations Should Erect Their Chapels

A missionary tells us that in one section of Colombia where fifteen missionaries are stationed, "at least one hundred and fifty preaching points are visited each month. Over one-third of these centers have built their own place of worship, leaving of course the majority of the services to be held in private homes. The twenty-five part-time and full-time native preachers, who make monthly rounds, receive no salary but support themselves (and in some cases their families) by manual labor and the small offerings their people give them. Two of our congregations are taking on the support of native preachers, and we trust that others will be doing the same soon.

"But let us ask: How many churches or school buildings would the native Christians have built if the Mission had started doing it for them? Answer: None. When would the native Church grow to support their own pastors if the Mission would do it for them? Answer: Never. . . .

"The native church left to its own, of course has

to suffer; it has to struggle and sometimes its efforts seem so feeble, we feel sorry and want to help. The result, however, would be the same as the effect produced by the preacher who helped what would have become a beautiful butterfly from its cocoon. He watched impatiently the great and seemingly futile effort to emerge, until his good but misunderstanding heart could stand it no longer; so with his sharp penknife he cut a few of the silken cords at the mouth of the encasement. Struggling ceased and there burst forth—a shapeless, weak, helpless, ugly mass to live but a moment.... A rule of life had been violated. Left to itself, after much writhing, contortion and labor, a well-formed strong and beautifully colored creature would have come forth.... A bamboo house with a straw roof and mud walls, built with native money and full of people is better than a beautiful brick and cement structure built with foreign funds that has but a half-dozen in the congregation....

"No money for native preachers and native churches is not a handicap nor hindrance; it is a challenge to missionary ability, and a policy that, if adopted generally and more rigidly, would save many a heartache and produce a stronger, more humble church in the foreign field." [*]

Fourth, the pastor needs to feel that his responsibility is to his congregation rather than to the Mission. Quite naturally the Mission-paid worker is responsible to the Mission, if it is paying his salary. As long as he has the approval of the missionary, he has nothing to fear. The pastor who is not supported by the Mission, but chosen and maintained by the congregation feels his responsibility to his flock. The congregation will also feel a closer tie with its pastor. The pastor will see that if he is to better his condition,

---

[*] William Shillingsburn in *The Pilot.*

even financially, he must build up his church. This interdependence is most salutary for both pastor and church.

Fifth, the spirit of faith and sacrifice required on the part of the worker helps develop a vigorous spiritual ministry. It is spiritually healthy for the pastor to be obliged to trust God for his support. The missionary can stunt a worker's spiritual growth by depriving him of the necessity of depending upon God. A worker is not likely to develop that rugged and robust character, so necessary to a spiritual ministry, if the missionary constantly defends him from the struggle by supplying his needs. The Mission-supported worker learns to bring each new financial problem to the missionary. He is the source of his income. When he marries, when a baby is born, when there is illness, he comes to present his need to the missionary. This cannot but have a withering effect on the worker's moral and spiritual character.

Mission Support Weakens Workers

Workers who are lacking in the faith and stamina required by the rigors of a life of dependence upon God will soon eliminate themselves from the list of workers. Under the system of Mission-support, they might continue drawing their salary for years, and thus constitute an element of spiritual weakness in the church.

We have found this to be a fairly accurate "Gideon's test" to distinguish between those who are truly called of God, and those who lack that call. Any effort to hold through financial means a worker, who without financial help would not continue in the ministry, is certain to weaken the indigenous church. What is more, it hinders the spiritual growth of the worker himself.

States one of our missionaries: "Pastors receiving outside aid have in many instances grown lazy and remained aloof from the financial problems of their churches. An instance developed only recently in a small church in _____. A pastor who had been receiving foreign assistance was asked to take charge of two small church groups, thereby receiving aid from both churches and attaining a fair degree of financial independence from foreign funds. This pastor thought the matter over for a while, rather disliked the extra work involved in caring for two churches instead of one, and finally wrote a letter refusing to care for more than one church. From this one instance, which could be multiplied many times, it can be observed that the continued acceptance of foreign assistance kills even evangelistic incentive."

Sixth, in the end the worker is better off financially without Mission support. When a worker receives even a portion of his support from the Mission, it almost invariably means that the members of his congregation will not assume the proper responsbility for his support. They consider that he receives a salary. It may be that he actually receives only one-third of the amount that he needs, yet it is enough to keep them from feeling personally responsible.

The funds that a Mission has at its disposal for the support of national workers are usually limited, and as a result are spread out too thinly to care adequately for the workers. As a result the worker fails to receive sufficient support either from the Mission or from his congregation. When some of our national workers have been cut off completely from the help of the Mission and their congregations have become aware that they are entirely responsible for the support of their pastor, the workers have found that in not too long a time, their income is better than when they were subsidized by the Mission.

Also there is likely to be better feeling between the worker and the missionary. Usually the allowances are not adequate, and so, as the worker suffers he may unconsciously build up resentment against the missionary, feeling that he should do something to relieve his distress. But when the worker ceases to consider the missionary as an employer and recognizes his own ministry as a God-given responsibility, his whole outlook toward the work and the missionary is favorably affected.

Seventh, self-support places the national worker in an advantageous position with his countrymen. Mission-paid workers have been accused of being spies for a foreign power, and the monthly check has been used as evidence against them. Some workers have been put to death or are in concentration camps because of this. As the spirit of nationalism grows, and propaganda increases against "Yankee imperialism," we shall need increasingly to safeguard our national workers and churches against the possibilities of such false accusations. In Latin America, the priests often tell the people that missionaries are paid by Wall Street, and are the forerunners of political and economic domination by the "Colossus of the North." Naturally, then, Mission-paid workers may easily be considered agents of a foreign power. When one of our missionaries had occasion to explain to an official of the American Embassy in his country that our churches are self-governing and self-supporting, this man remarked: "I am delighted to hear this. If all Missions would work on that principle it would save our department a good many headaches."

Even when a Mission-paid worker is not accused of being a political agent of a foreign power, he may still be considered the agent of a *foreign* religion, preaching a foreign doctrine *because he is paid for it.* His countrymen will question his sincerity.

Writing of North Africa, J. J. Cooksey ° declares, "The day of big things (for Christianity) . . . will

---

° *In the Land of the Vanished Church.*

come, if ever, when Islam can see men, members of
its own household, who, undirected by an alien
Western organization, unpaid by foreign missionary
funds, will spend themselves and their all for their
faith, and be ready to seal it with their blood. . . .
The employed native Christian agent makes the
Moslem smile in the beard; the foreign missionary
he indulgently tolerates. He will only furiously think
. . . when Christ really and utterly captures some
Moslem heart in sacrificial power, fills it with His
Spirit, and consecrates it for the task of building an
indigenous North African Christianity."

To understand how the receiving of a salary paid
from foreign funds affects a Christian worker's standing in the eyes of his compatriots, let us reverse the
picture. How would we feel about one of our neighbors who would receive a salary from some "Moslem
Mission" of Arabia to distribute literature and make
converts for Islam among us? Would we be deeply
convinced of his sincerity? On the other hand, the
man who from deep conviction and at the cost of
great personal sacrifices preaches his doctrine, without remuneration from a foreign source, has no such
handicap to overcome.

*Eighth, self-support opens the door to unlimited
expansion.* One of the most discouraging aspects of
depending on foreign funds for the support of pastors
and churches, is that it automatically limits the
church's capacity for extension. For example, if a
missionary receives, let us say, $100 monthly for the
work in his area, it will not be long until every cent
of it will be allocated. From then on every new worker
places an additional strain on the budget. Every new
church requires additional funds. The missionary appeals for extra help so that he can enter the open doors
before him, but the Mission Board must reply that
funds are not available. Such a notice is equivalent
to saying, "Do not open any more outstations, or

found any more churches. Do not encourage any more converts to enter the ministry. We cannot provide the funds for additional activities." Surely God would not place His messenger in such a ridiculous predicament. This situation is avoided when the missionary does not depend on foreign funds for the maintenance of the work. The indigenous church has no such limitations placed upon it, for it draws from the country itself and, as it expands, finds within itself the means for its own support.

Having summarized the principal factors that make the self-support of the national church imperative, we shall see how this goal may be attained.

The "How" of Self-Support

If we are to attain self-support, it is important that we lay the right foundation from the very beginning of the work, since the procedures we establish with the first few converts in founding the first church, will doubtless become the pattern to be followed by the converts and churches which will spring up later in the district.

It may be objected that if we start mentioning money at the very beginning, we shall make a bad impression on the people. In Latin America, for example, the priests are always asking for money, so, to prove that the Protestants are different, some missionaries and national workers have gone to the other extreme. They never mention the question of finance or take up an offering, at least in the first months or even years of the work. The fact that the subject has been abused does not free us from our obligation to give the correct teaching and establish wholesome practices.

It is much easier to teach a convert his financial obligations to the work of God during the first few weeks after his conversion, than it is to do so after he has been a member of the church for ten years. He will see no reason why he should begin then, after he has enjoyed the privilege of salvation and membership

for so long without it. So the time to start is while the
converts are still young in the faith. If their lives have
received the touch of the Spirit of God, they will
respond to the challenge of carrying their own proper
share of the load.

Converts should know what is to be expected of
them before they are accepted as members of the
church. Our Central American pastors teach the new
converts that they should pay tithes, even before
they are baptized in water. There is no advantage in
Teach accepting converts as members of the church who
Converts have no intention of fulfilling the duties of an ordinary
to Tithe Christian. Let us not be afraid that they will slip
away if we teach them their responsibilities. It is
better to build a little more slowly and lay a proper
foundation, than to build more quickly and find out
afterwards that the work cannot progress for lack of
a proper beginning. Once the foundation is laid, the
growth will be solid and the benefits of the increased
blessings upon the work will more than repay for the
time required to give the necessary teaching at the
beginning.

Sometimes the enthusiasm with which the converts respond to an appeal surprises us. We have
seen them enter into the spirit of hilarious giving,
donating land, labor and materials for church buildings. Churches have given hundreds of pounds of
corn and beans for the support of Bible students,
and others have given the "widow's mite," in their
poverty sacrificing literally all they have in order to
see the work of God prosper. The liberality of these
converts has been a source of amazement to visitors.
God honors faith, and we need to believe that He will
work in the hearts of His people along the line of
self-support, just as we believe that His Spirit will
stir up the believers to respond to any other phase
of gospel truth. Here as elsewhere in the spiritual

realm, the law is: "According to your faith be it unto you."

In a pioneer work, unless the national evangelist receives help from neighboring churches, it may be necessary for him to find some secular employment until the church is fully established. Of course, a full-time ministry is better, as a worker is then free to give more time to his spiritual task. But a minister who must work with his hands to support himself and his family, temporarily, is to be preferred to one who is dependent on foreign funds for his support. The example of the Apostle Paul can be safely followed in this case (Acts 20:35; 18:3). °

Pioneer Workers Support Themselves

Probably the standard procedure followed by most missionaries in opening a work in a new town is open to criticism. The accepted method seems to be to pick out a town that needs a church, then rent a hall, furnish it with seats, etc., hang up a sign, "Gospel Hall," or its equivalent, and start preaching services. The first night's audience will likely be composed mostly of children. These disappear after

---

° A word of caution should be given. While it is commendable for a worker to support himself by secular employment during the pioneer stages of a work, yet it is harmful for the worker to continue to do so after that the church is established. Then his sacrifice is not a blessing but a hindrance, for the congregation is permitted to shirk its rightful responsibility. This results in the loss of spiritual blessing and vision. The church is robbed of the fruits of a full-time ministry. Furthermore it will be difficult for any other worker to follow in the pastorate, since the congregation probably will demand that he, too, support himself.

The ministry of the worker is adversely affected also. Robbed of time for study and prayer, he is unable to "feed the flock." He has little time for visiting his members. Tired after a day's work in the field or shop, he cannot give his best to the mid-week services. The whole church suffers.

Then, too, secular work may become a snare to a worker, tempting him to leave the ministry entirely. It has happened!

Every established church should support its own pastor. Workers should be encouraged to devote their full time to the ministry from the time that the church is set in order.

the priest (in Latin America) has visited the parents and told them to keep their children away from the services.

Thus prejudice is built up from the very beginning. The missionary is a foreigner, preaching a foreign religion. The cost of everything is paid by him. Later on, when converts are won, they will see no reason for taking over the financial responsibility for the work. From the beginning the missionary supplied everything. Why should he not continue to do so?

To avoid these mistakes, it is better that the missionary get acquainted with the people of the vicinity before starting to preach in a designated place of worship. Let him make friends with the neighbors. In their homes he may introduce them to songs or choruses and explain the Scriptures without any formal religious service. Then when interest is sufficient to require a public service, the missionary can suggest that one of those interested open up his home.

It is preferable not to begin regular meetings in the missionary's own home. He may explain that the neighbors will be much more willing to come to another's home than to his own. Someone may offer his front room, or all may go together to rent a large room which can accommodate the people. In such circumstances, they will all feel the responsibility of sharing expenses.

As the missionary travels over the district, visiting towns and villages, he will be constantly on the lookout for people who are friendly to the gospel message. He will endeavor to establish services in their homes. This method is fruitful for the missionary, and even better for the national worker, since the people come to accept their responsibility for the work, and are not likely to consider the missionary or worker as a source of financial aid. Following this plan, it is possible to open up work in a town without resorting to the initiative-killing expedient of having the Mission pay all the bills and permitting the new converts to become accustomed to Mission support.

The following account illustrates this point. °

Opening New Work Illustrated

"One of our missionaries . . . began a new church in the village of her residence. . . . The first problem that faced her was a meeting place. The small handful of Christians naturally looked to the missionary's residence, for it was perhaps more commodious than any of their homes. The missionary, however, said, "No." They must provide a place for themselves. This seemed harsh and unsympathetic, but it drove the Christians to become resourceful and to consider the solution of their problems without the benefit of the missionary and the missionary's resources. They found a place and therefore the transition from the missionary's home to another place was never necessary. Had they begun to meet in the home of the missionary, they would have been satisfied to stay there indefinitely. Today these Christians have not only rented their church building, but have begun to build their own place of worship.

"The next problem was chairs for use during the service. No Christian had enough chairs in his home, so they immediately turned to the missionary. . . . Again the missionary said No. It did look as though the missionary was not willing to share, but it was a problem for which the church must find a solution, and it did.

"The next item that came up for consideration was a light for the evening meetings. They used very small lamps or wicks burning in dishes of oil. These lights, of course, are only good for a general breaking of the darkness in a room or for one individual to use

---

° From a paper *A Study of Indigenous Policies and Procedures,* published by the Conservative Baptist Foreign Missions Society.

in reading. Again they turned to the missionary, for
she had the only adequate light. The missionary gave
in and allowed them to use her light. Months passed;
in fact a year passed. The missionary's remark is most
enlightening: 'And who provided the oil for that
lamp? The missionary, of course. Did not the lamp
belong to the missionary? Therefore the missionary
must provide the oil.' Thus we see that when the missionary finally did give in . . . this giving in was the
entrance for the Christians to use something belong-
ing to the missionary. So until the missionary left,
the Christians used not only the lamp but the oil of
the missionary.

"These things may seem very small. One could
condemn the missionary as heartless and indifferent
for refusing to share with the Christians. If we investigate further, however, we realize the wisdom of
the missionary in insisting that the church depend on
its own resources, and to look to itself for the solution
of its own problems. Had the missionary opened
her house and provided chairs, the time would
come when the missionary would leave and the Christians would have been unprepared to assume these
simple responsibilities. Not only would they be unprepared, they would still be weak, for whatever the
missionary does (in giving financial aid) encourages
the Christians to remain babes as far as assuming responsibility is concerned. They would not have the
privilege of doing things which would strengthen them
in their own organic life. The Christians become resourceful and strong in the solution of these matters
only as they are given responsibility. The wise move,
and in fact the New Testament procedure, is to have
the Christians undertake these things themselves from
the very beginning."

RETHINK THIS CHAPTER

1. Although a church be self-supporting, how may it come short of being truly indigenous?
2. What are the dangers in the use of foreign funds?
3. Does the modern method of supporting national pastors and erecting church buildings for the local congregations have the backing of scriptural example?
4. Explain how a tithing church can support its pastor even though the congregation be very poor.
5. Should pastors of a national church live on the American standard?
6. How does self-support affect the spiritual life of a congregation?
7. Is it a hindrance to the spiritual development of a church when it must struggle with financial problems?
8. How does self-support affect the relationship between pastor and congregation?
9. What is the usual effect upon the spiritual life of a worker who becomes accustomed to depending upon the missionary for his support?
10. Show that Mission support may even hinder a worker financially.
11. Explain the handicap in which a Mission-supported worker is placed, relative to his countrymen.
12. How does Mission support hinder expansion?
13. Explain the importance of teaching new converts to support the work while they are still young in the way.
14. How should a national be supported while pioneering a new work?
15. What weaknesses result in following the usual method of opening a new work?
16. How may these weaknesses be avoided?
17. How may a missionary make a new work self-supporting from the beginning?

7

The National Organization

Having discussed the establishment of the local church, we will now consider how such churches may be bound together; for the *churches* should become the *Church*. In this we are following the New Testament pattern. The Apostle Paul referred to the churches of a province as a unit—as the churches of Macedonia, of Achaia or of Judea (2 Cor. 8:1; 9:2; 1 Thess. 2:14). The same bonds that united the individual Christians in the local church, united these local churches into the CHURCH.

Churches Need to Be Bound Together

Just as individual believers need the fellowship and ministry of other Christians, so the local church needs to recognize that it forms a part of *the* Church and especially of that part of the Church which is in their own district or province. The necessity for such union arises from the following factors:

First, the need for Christian fellowship. Small groups of individual believers that are cut off from all contact with other churches tend to become discouraged and inactive. Christian fellowship revives the courage of the believers, brings joy in the Holy Ghost, and stimulates Christian activity.

Second, Christian unity and fellowship provide a stabilizing and corrective influence upon local congregations. Just as an individual Christian, left to his own devices, may take up strange notions and interpretations of the Scripture, or embrace fanciful or fanatical ideas, so congregations also are open to the same danger. Unity and fellowship tend to correct wrong tendencies. Contact with other churches serves to preserve a spiritual balance in the local congregation.

Third, over-all organization permits the carrying out of specific projects that would be impossible for the local church alone. These projects include the evangelization of unreached sections, the establishing of training centers for Christian workers, and the election and support of qualified overseers, evangelists, and teachers who will carry out the projects necessary for the maintenance and advancement of the work.

It has already been pointed out that it is unwise to begin any national organization before there are local churches and national ministers, since any organization that begins with the missionaries will be essentially foreign in character.° Americans must not permit their natural love for organization to cause the organization to become an end in itself. The end must always be the establishing and strengthening of the indigenous church, and organization must be kept subservient to that goal.

When there are from three to five churches in a province, it is time to bring representatives of each local church together for fellowship and discussion. In Central America we call these meetings "conferences." In El Salvador, the first such gathering had eleven churches represented, but in the other republics, there were not more than four churches established when we called the first "conference." The organization of these conferences is patterned in general after a District Council of the Assemblies of God in the U.S.A. except that, while the national

°See footnote, p. 24

organizations recognize the spiritual ties which bind them to brethren of like precious faith in other lands, each conference is sovereign.

Geographical features, political boundaries, differences of language, and transportation facilities will determine the size of the district to be embraced as a conference or council. There is little to be gained by trying to bind churches together into a single unit when they are far removed from each other and no actual fellowship can be maintained. When distance, language or political barriers make it impractical to unite the churches into one district, it is advisable to divide the district into smaller units with a sectional conference or council in each area.

In much the same way that the charter members of a local church reach agreement as to the standards for their local church,° so the churches should come together to discuss the basis for the development of the Church in their area. The local churches are represented by their pastors and duly elected delegates. Other Christians from the congregations may be present as observers. These conferences become the annual business meeting for directing the work of the district.

Sectional Presbyters

As the work extends, the district is divided into sections. Each section may have from five to ten local churches. These churches may meet together in a fellowship meeting every three to six months, as circumstances permit. An overseer, or presbyter, chosen at the annual conference of all the churches, takes the oversight of each section and helps the pastors and churches in the problems that arise. Since the presbyter is also a pastor of one of the churches in the section, he will not need to be supported from other sources. But for the same reason, the number

---

°See p. 26

of churches under his supervision should be limited in number, else he will either neglect his church in caring for the section, or will be unable to oversee the work properly.

The general officials, such as superintendent, secretary and treasurer are elected by the general assembly at the annual meeting. It is probable that the nationals will desire a missionary to fill the office of superintendent until the nationals are trained in the management of the church. However, as national leaders develop, all official positions should be filled by them. From the point where the national brethren become able to fill various offices, to the point where they can take over the entire administration, is but a step. It is best that they do so while there are still missionaries of experience on the field to guide them. It is poor policy to wait until the missionaries are suddenly withdrawn and leadership is forced upon the nationals.

The providing of leadership for the national church is just as much a part of missionary work as is the winning of converts. To accomplish this, the missionary must be willing to step aside, working unobtrusively as the administration passes into the hands of others.

The willingness of the missionary to cooperate with national leaders is a test both of his humility and of the quality of his missionary passion. As one national minister expressed it: "Many missionaries are willing to serve under the District Council (composed of missionaries) but not under the local committees (with nationals).... Unless our missionary friends can extricate themselves from this superiority complex, we are afraid that they will not have much fruitful ministry in our land."

Some Missions have two organizations for each field: one composed only of missionaries, the other composed only of nationals. This may be satisfactory if the missionary organization limits its scope to those matters which affect missionaries only, but if the missionary organization is to act as a supreme court and place limitations on the national organization, reserving the right of approving or disapproving all resolutions passed by the nationals, and the power of veto on questions that affect the churches and the national ministry, then the system would be liable to a serious breakdown.

A Separate Organization for Missionaries?

I believe that it makes for unity if we have only one body representing the field; i.e., only one body with power to make decisions which affect the national work. ° That body should be composed of representatives from the local churches, the national ministers and the missionaries. The missionaries may lend their strength and counsel to the work in the early stages and even fill executive positions until such a time as national leaders are prepared to take over this responsibility. Only let the missionary be sure to recognize the proper time to step aside, permitting the nationals to fill these posts.

Someone may object. But if the missionaries are allowed a voice in the national organization, they will completely control it, and there will be, in effect, no national organization. In such instances, one of the following circumstances may be to blame, and should be corrected: *First,* perhaps the work has been organized on a national scale too soon with the missionaries outnumbering the nationals; *second,* there may be too many missionaries in that particular area for the good of the indigenous church (a redistribution of missionary personnel is required),

---

° This statement is not intended to discourage the forming of an organization of missionaries in order to deal with their own special problems. Such an organization is often a necessity. However, it should limit its decisions to the sphere of missionary activity, and not undertake to dictate to the national organization.

or *third*, something is woefully wanting in the method used to develop national workers (the missionaries need to reexamine their system).

Since the churches are to have a national organization, some thought must be given to providing financial support for the officials who will serve them. How this will be done depends largely upon whether the offices are considered full-time posts. If not, the superintendent and other officials will retain their pastorates and will travel over the field to visit the churches only in special times of need. Ordinary problems can be handled by the presbyter of each section. It must be said that this plan has much in its favor, inasmuch as it does not place a financial load upon the churches and tends to avoid the danger of a top-heavy, overcentralized, national organization.

On the other hand, experience has taught us that a tremendous load is often placed upon the official that must pastor a church and take care of district duties also; so that the office of superintendent at least is usually a full-time post.

In Central America, the pastors support their officials by sending in to the central office the tithe of their own incomes. Some Conferences augment this through special offerings taken by each church, or by tithing the other church income (outside of that which is given to the support of the pastor), as may be agreed upon by the Conference.

RETHINK THIS CHAPTER

1. What can be said in favor of organizing the churches of a district into a Council or Conference?
2. How may this organization begin?
3. What factors may determine the size of the area to be embraced in a Council?
4. Explain the functions of a sectional presbyter.
5. Who will fill the offices of the national organization?

6. Discuss the advisability of having a missionary organization separate from the national organization.
7. What are the probable faults in the manner of developing the national organization when the missionaries can completely dominate it?
8. How may the officials of the organization be supported?

8

Converting to Indigenous Church Methods

A missionary once remarked to the author, "Starting an indigenous work in a pioneer field is not the major difficulty. What we would most like to know is how to go about converting to indigenous church methods on a field where the work has been carried on for years under the old mission-compound system."

The conversion of a work from a nonindigenous basis to methods which will permit the development of an indigenous church is probably one of the most difficult tasks that a missionary can undertake. Doubtless it would be impossible to make hard-and-fast rules, adequate for every field. Conditions differ widely. In some places present-day missionaries have fallen heir to a work founded by their predecessors. This work includes a staff of considerable size and a subsidy of Mission funds for its support. We can here make only some general suggestions as to possible steps in this conversion, urging that at the same time all missionaries concerned should read books on the subject and study indigenous procedure with a sincere desire to find the proper solution. We trust that the Holy Spirit shall guide both individual missionaries and the administrative staff in taking adequate steps.

Missionaries should not be impatient with nationals who seem slow in changing to the indigenous plan. Rather, they should realize that existing conditions are largely due to wrong training and practice. We must therefore patiently correct our own errors and endeavor to return to the New Testament pattern.

J. Herbert Kane points out ° that the vast majority of churches on the foreign field have gotten off to a wrong start and that it will not be an easy matter to change after thirty or forty years of unscriptural practice. "Our plans therefore must be carefully conceived, and wisely executed. In this connection, there are three important principles which we must ever bear in mind.

General Principles

"In the first place, *they (the nationals) must be allowed to frame their own policies.* Most missionaries today are in favor of the indigenous church in principle; but when it comes to working out the details, they are guilty of backseat driving. They relinquish the wheel but insist on directing the way. This is a serious mistake. . . .

"Secondly, *we must permit them to develop along their own lines.* The churches of the East should be allowed to develop their own peculiar type of Christianity. It is not necessary for them to adopt our style of architecture, our order of service, our methods of work, or even our form of government. . . . We must remember that while it is right to make a Christian out of a Moslem, it is wrong to make an American out of a Chinese.

"And last, but not least, *they should be allowed to proceed at their own pace.* Many a fine missionary has broken his health and his heart trying to speed up the people of the East. It cannot be done; so the missionary, if he is wise, will come to this conclusion early in his ministry, and thereafter act accordingly. . . . 'First the blade, then the ear, after that the full corn in the ear.' Our difficulty comes when we want all three in the first ten days. We must be as patient in

---

° *In Two-Fold Growth.*

the building of the church as Jesus was in the training
of the twelve.... "We, too, must be patient—infinitely
patient—with the church leaders when they fail to
adopt some pet scheme of ours, or when they hesitate
to exercise discipline, or when they omit to send in the
annual report. We must not be surprised if they are
late for Sunday service, or forget about the deacons'
meeting, or arrive three days late for Bible school.
These are the traits which will require many years
... for them to overcome."

As *a first step* toward conversion to indigenous
principles, I would suggest that all the missionaries
in the area gather together for discussion, with the
aim of outlining a practical plan of procedure. All
missionaries concerned should be present, for it is
very important that there be harmony of spirit and
purpose in taking these steps. Even when all agree as
to the ultimate goal, there still may be sharp differences of opinion as to the methods to be employed in reaching that goal. Such differences of
opinion may constitute a serious obstacle to the
realization of the plan of conversion. Therefore time
spent in prayer and honest discussion in order to
reach agreement is well worthwhile. Patience must
be manifested by all, since it is not easy for a person
with years of experience in missionary work to change
his viewpoint or his methods. Plenty of time should be
allowed for a change of thinking to take place. All the
problems will not be solved in one session, nor perhaps even in one series of sessions. Though progress
seems slow, missionaries may take heart by reminding
themselves that the project is not simply a pet scheme,
but is backed up by the Word of God, by the foreign
missionary policy of the sponsoring board, and by the
Spirit of God who is most certainly leading us in this
direction. He will honor New Testament procedure,

direct us in the steps we should take and enable us to iron out our differences. So, "If God be for us. . . !"

It may be necessary to make temporary concessions in order not to disrupt the established work. The unknown and different factors on each field make it unwise to lay down inflexible rules. Each missionary is a member of Christ's body, and the Holy Spirit will surely guide each one into all truth when there is a sincere desire to do His will. All missionaries will doubtless agree to the proposal that at least all the new work shall be established on indigenous principles. Those missionaries who are desirous of converting the established work can trust that the blessings from the new works will overflow into the established churches. Perhaps then those in charge will see that they are missing great blessings and be more ready to make the change.

Inspire National Workers
Taking it for granted that the missionaries *are* in favor of following indigenous principles, *the next step* will be to prepare the nationals for the changes to come by showing them the advantages and importance of indigenous methods. Again patient teaching and discussion will be required. As missionaries, we are largely responsible for their viewpoint. We have trained them in dependence upon us. We shall have to retrain them in independence and initiative.

Some missionaries have themselves reached the decision that the work should become indigenous, and have tried to make it so by simply announcing that from that time on, the work was to be self-supporting. They have then precipitately cut off the support of the workers. But there is much more to the problem than merely cutting off a worker from financial support. The initiative for evangelism and leadership must spring from within the national's own spirit. This requires time to develop. It is comparable to the process that changes a boy into a man. The parent

instructs, counsels and guides his son, all the while
increasing the responsibility upon him and allowing
more liberty in decisions until the time comes that
the son is capable of making his own way. Contrari-
wise, we have made the mistake of training the national workers in dependence. We must therefore take
steps at once to convert to indigenous principles, but
we must give the nationals a period of time in which
they may find their own feet. Otherwise they will be
left in the difficult circumstance of a boy who suddenly becomes an orphan.

Some of the more fainthearted and less aggressive
spirits among the workers may view the idea of
conversion to national leadership and responsibility
with considerable alarm. Having all their life depended on a salary from the Mission, it will require
courage and faith to step out without that support.
Some workers have been so fearful of being left without the financial backing of the Mission that they
have failed to adopt the suggestions of the missionary. They have not encouraged the local congregation to do its best in giving for fear that their
salary would be cut off.

One missionary relates how the Mission, in order to
encourage self-support, offered to match the amount
given to the pastor by the local congregation up to
the maximum of four pounds. Above this amount the
foreign funds would be cut back in proportion to
increased local offerings.

"Imagine our surprise when in only a month or two
practically every pastor had increased local offerings
as much as two or three pounds so that he might receive the maximum of foreign matching. . . . Imagine
our further surprise as time passed when we observed
that these local pastors held their church giving at this
peak without endeavoring to carry it on further still to
financial independence."

This instance reveals how necessary it is that the

nationals shall catch the vision themselves. It will be next to impossible for a missionary to develop a self-supporting church if the worker in charge is not in sympathy with the idea.

However, it is likely that it will be less difficult to convince the nationals of the benefits of the indigenous method than some missionaries suppose. In fact, the missionary may well be surprised at the eagerness with which the nationals grasp the possibilities. As they become inspired with the vision of evangelism through national initiative and see the opportunities for leadership which a truly indigenous work offers, they will thrill to the joy of spiritual self-fulfillment. *Most workers will make greater sacrifices and dedicate themselves more fully to the work of God when inspired by the opportunity of filling a vital place in the Church of God than they will for the sake of a mere salary.*

The third step is to accompany the teaching with appropriate action. The long-range indigenous program calls for the development of all the ministries which the church requires—pastors, teachers, evangelists, and executives. All must be supplied from among the converts themselves, and all phases of the national church must become completely self-supporting. In the transition period from a Mission-supported and directed work to a completely indigenous church, it may be necessary to adopt certain temporary measures. We may not be able to change over completely with one stroke.

Planning for Financial Independence

In adopting temporary measures, we must not become discouraged with the main plan, nor lose sight of the goal. We must continue to pray, teach and believe. *Also we must beware lest temporary measures become permanent policies.* Our objective must be unalterable, but the methods may be fluid, to be revised from time to time to meet the exigencies of changing conditions. One reason why it may sometimes be necessary to stop short, temporarily, of our final goal, is to enable our national brethren to come along with us in our thinking. The very principles of the indigenous church require that they think for themselves, so it is understood that the steps to be taken should have the general approval of the nationals themselves. °

An initial action which might readily obtain the approval of all should be a "hold-the-line" policy as to the use of foreign funds for the support of national workers. In other words, having taken the wrong road, we will proceed in that direction no further. We will henceforth seek to meet the needs that arise in the work from national sources, without employing additional foreign funds. Following this, steps should be taken to develop local sources for the support of workers which heretofore have been dependent on Mission funds. Each organized church should become responsible for the support of its pastor. This means that we teach indigenous principles to the local congregations.

Teach Local Congregations

If the churches have not been properly organized with their own official board and pastor, this should be done according to the procedure already explained. °° After teaching and explaining, we may hold business sessions with the board and with the entire church, urging them to come to some conclusion

---

° It might be noted here that since Mission funds come from Mission sources, it is not within the jurisdiction of the nationals to determine the amount of foreign funds which may be used in the work. The missionaries, since they are the ones who are held responsible, will determine this. Once funds are made available for the work, the nationals may be consulted as to how they may best be used. However, this particular condition, which results from the process of conversion, is abnormal. The necessity of allocating foreign funds for the maintenance of pastors or churches will disappear as the work attains the goal of self-support.

°° See pp. 25-33

concerning the support of their pastor. In some cases
it may be necessary to give them a little time for study
and decision. The date of complete responsibility may
be postponed for three to six months. Or we may soften
the blow somewhat by reducing the present salary of
the worker, perhaps one-third every three months,
until he is completely dependent upon the church for
support. This last suggestion has its disadvantages,
however, since sometimes the church fails to respond
until it knows that its pastor is completely dependent
upon the members. The procedure has been likened to
cutting off a dog's tail an inch at a time so that it won't
hurt so much! Nevertheless the plan has been suc-
cessfully worked out in numerous instances.

If we have a choice, it is preferable to use foreign
funds to aid the struggling local church with the
rent of their building, temporarily, or in the construction of their church, rather than to help in the matter
of the pastor's salary. When we must continue to
assist in the matter of the pastor's salary for a time,
it is better to pay the money into the local church
treasury, thus permitting the pastor to receive the
help from the church treasury rather than from the
Mission directly. This tends to avoid the idea that the
worker is supported by the Mission. It also makes for a
healthier relationship between pastor and congregation.

Helping a Needy Worker

It is recognized that occasions do arise when it is
a duty to succor a needy brother. In such cases, it is
not only the duty of the missionary, but of the whole
Christian constituency, to help. Why should the missionary alone assume the responsibility of showing
Christian charity? Should not the members of the
church and neighboring congregations as well respond
to the need of a brother in distress? Usually if the
matter is brought to their attention, they will gladly
help a truly worthy brother. The missionary, as a
brother in Christ, may also share in this gift. In such

cases of pressing need, it is better to make an outright gift in order to help a worker through the crisis, rather than to promise him a monthly allowance. On the former plan he can thank God for supplying his need and continue on his way in faith, anticipating that God will care for him.

Fourth, the national leaders themselves should have a say as to how money available for the development and the maintenance of the work is to be used. This is particularly true of money that comes from local sources. Such questions as to which evangelist should be chosen for a certain task, and how much help he is to receive while carrying out his commission are certainly questions which the missionary should not decide. The executive board should make such decisions. This board should include a sufficient number of nationals so that the voice of the national church can be heard. The missionary thus avoids unfavorable criticism. At least criticisms are less severe when the nationals share this responsibility with the missionary. It is an important step in the right direction when the national brethren are given a voice as to the distribution of funds.

The final step in converting from a Mission-supported work to a self-supporting work, is to place the entire responsibility for the *maintenance of the work* on the national churches. For some time afterward, the Mission may still share with the national churches the tasks of evangelizing new territory, the training of workers, literature publication, etc., but eventually even these responsibilities will be borne by the nationals.

Conversion Completed

To illustrate the general process, I shall relate some of our own experiences as we went through the struggle of changing from a Mission-supported work to the indigenous church methods in a certain field where we served early in our missionary ministry. Certainly I do not present ourselves as models for others to follow. My wife and I were inexperienced in missionary work, but certain factors did favor us: We had a firm conviction that the indigenous principles pointed the way to victory, and since we were the only Assemblies of God missionaries in the country, we did not have to battle with divided opinions on the part of the missionary staff.

The work on this field was small but not new. Upon arrival, we found four small churches and four workers. Two of these workers were receiving support directly from Mission headquarters in the U.S.A. since there had been no resident missionary there for a number of years. The other two were new workers, who looked forward to receiving some help as soon as a missionary might again be stationed on the field. In the meantime, the workers who were supported, generously helped the two who received no help, giving them tithes and offerings from their own allowances.

From the very first, we began to place emphasis on the necessity of the work becoming self-supporting. We organized the groups that had not been set in order, encouraging them to become self-governing. We also endeavored to inspire those converts in the churches who felt a call to the work of God, to step out in faith. They began to respond to our plea, but did not take seriously our ideas about the work becoming self-supporting. They thought that it was an idealistic dream, and that given time, we would begin to dole out Mission funds to support the workers as the former missionary had done. All other Missionary Societies, operating in that country, were doing the same thing.

The number of volunteers grew until there were about ten full-time or part-time workers, two of them supported by funds from the U.S.A. and the others either dependent on what their congregations could supply, or working part time in order to exist. The inequality was too apparent. I had determined, however, not to proceed any farther along the road of designating Mission funds for the support of workers, for I realized that the indigenous principles presented the only road to spiritual prosperity for the work. In the meantime, the workers waited more or less patiently for me to wake up and give them the help they needed.

One day one of the workers who received support from the Mission, told me of the need of one of the brethren and dropped a broad hint that it was time to help him financially. "I just told him to be patient," he said, "Brother Hodges is just waiting to see your faithfulness and when he is sure that you are going to be a good worker, he will ask for support from the Mission for you." So they nursed the hope that better days would come.

Finally after a little more than a year, the crisis occurred. Upon our first visit to the field, with the aid of a more experienced missionary, we had brought the churches together to form a Conference. The storm broke at the second anniversary of the Conference. I was presiding at a business session, when one of the newer workers arose and said: "Brother, my family is suffering. I have several children. I cannot continue in the work unless I can have the promise of regular monthly support." With that he came forward and handed to me his license to preach. Others followed him, one by one, though in a less dramatic manner. With the exception of four, the workers said that they could not continue. One of these four—he received support from the Mission—tried to exhort the discontented to faithfulness. The others remained silent.

The Crisis

I lifted my heart to God for guidance. This was the decisive moment. Finally I said something like this: "Brethren, I feel deeply your need and your suffering. I will do all that I can to help you, but I

cannot promise a single worker a salary. The support
of the work must come from the country itself. Now if
the Mission has called you to preach, you can place
your resignation with the Mission. But if you are
called of God, it does no good to turn in your
resignation to me—you must answer to God. It is not
a question between you and me, but between you and
God. Are you called of God, or not?" Then I waited
with a prayer in my heart.

The brethren were all quiet for several moments.
Finally one of the leaders who received no help,
asked to say a word. "Brethren, I feel that we have
been hasty. I've gone through a lot, as have you.
We talk about trusting God, but I wonder if I have
ever really trusted God for my support. For my part,
I withdraw my resignation and state here that I am
going to put God to the test for one year."

Slowly, as God moved on their hearts, the others
stood up, one by one, to say that they would put God
to the test for another year. We didn't keep every
worker, but almost all of them remained with us. So
we entered the new year with renewed strength.

**All Workers
on Same
Footing**

But the battle was still far from won. I felt strongly
the matter of the financial inequality among the
workers, so I wrote a letter to our missionary secretary
asking for counsel. He answered somewhat as follows:
"I believe that we should take away the offerings from
the brethren who now receive designated support. We
shall give them six months time before this becomes
effective, in order for them to make the necessary
adjustments. Then we will place this same amount at
your disposal, so that you can help the brethren as you
see the need."

The two brethren concerned were then advised
that they would be receiving offerings from the Mission for only six months more, and that from then
on, all workers would be on the same footing. One of
them was a visiting worker from another Latin Ameri-

can country. When he found out that he would not receive his offering, he decided to return home. I did not dissuade him, not because I did not appreciate his labors, but I realized that we must build of national material, and unless he were willing to take his place with the rest of the pastors, his presence would not benefit the work. He returned to his own country and has done a good work for God there. The other worker took a manly attitude, making his plans so that within six months he had a little business going on the side to tide him over the crisis.

At the end of the six months, the money was sent to me, as agreed, rather than to the two workers. I shared with the national leaders of our Conference the responsibility for the distribution of these funds. During this time of transition, I traveled constantly, visiting the churches and encouraging them to support their own workers, endeavoring to establish tithing as the scriptural basis for giving to God's work. After some months, the worker who had been deprived of his offering testified as follows: "Brethren, you know that I felt that Brother Hodges had been quite severe with me when he arranged to have my offering taken away after I had served the Mission for so many years. But I saw that if I were to prosper, I must needs get busy and build up my church. So I have been working with my people, and now I am proud to say that I am not dependent upon the Mission, but I have developed my own church."

A few years later, after God had visited that field with revival and the number of workers had increased to more than twenty, it was my great joy to be with these workers in a Conference when the nationals themselves made a motion, and adopted the same, to the effect that *all* funds coming to the field from outside the country were to be used only for Bible school or evangelistic effort. No such funds were to be used for the support of pastors of established churches.

Nationals Vote Self-Support

Thus little by little, the idea had taken hold of them, and they had accepted it as basic and practical.

In that same meeting, one of the leaders was trying to make a point and by way of illustration said, "When Brother Hodges started to preach to us about a self-supporting church in _____, we thought that he was dreaming. We said that it could never be done. But he just kept hammering away, month after month, and now look at us—we, ourselves, have put this motion through. It has come from the workers, not the missionaries, and we are all glad for it."

RETHINK THIS CHAPTER

 1. Discuss three important general principles to be held in mind during the process of converting to indigenous principles.
 2. What is the first step to be taken in introducing indigenous methods in a work established on a nonindigenous basis?
 3. After agreement has been reached among the missionaries, what is the next step?
 4. Why may certain national workers be reluctant to push the introduction of indigenous church methods?
 5. Is it reasonable to expect the nationals to be enthusiastic about indigenous church principles? Explain your answer.
 6. What care must be taken when adopting temporary measures during the process of conversion?
 7. Discuss two such temporary measures.
 8. How may we best help the local church to get on its feet during its struggle to attain self-support?
 9. How may a worker who is in difficult economic circumstances be helped?
10. Should the nationals have a voice in the spending of local funds? Mission funds?
11. What points seem to you to be of special significance in the illustration which the author gives concerning his own experiences in introducing indigenous church methods in the work on his field?

9

Hindrances to Conversion to Indigenous Principles

Many of the well-established Missions are making a decided effort to introduce indigenous church principles into their mission work. Lessons dearly learned during World War II have convinced many missionaries that the indigenous way is the only way which brings lasting results. Even so, many Missions which profess to believe in these principles, as well as many missionaries who pay lip service to them, stop short of taking the necessary steps toward conversion, or "devolution," as the process of turning the reins of government into the hands of the nationals is sometimes called. Why the hesitancy? Let us examine some of the possible reasons.

First, perhaps unconsciously the missionary is reluctant to surrender the prestige and power which his present position affords. The man who is accustomed to having the decisive voice may find it difficult to turn over that authority to others, or to surrender title or position. Similarly, he may hesitate to relinquish his control of the purse strings. He knows that in his hands, money produces activity. It also gives authority to his voice in church matters. Perhaps without realizing what has taken place, he has come to have more faith in the results he can obtain by his use of money than he has in those results which the Holy Spirit can produce in the heart of the convert. "So long as policies (of self-support) are dictated by

Reluctance to Surrender Authority

considerations of convenience, there will be frequent
cases in which the immediate advantages of subsidy
will induce the missionary to depart from the harder
way.... The desirability of retaining influence over
the congregation by the power of the purse, of keeping hold of a promising worker, of maintaining the
status of the group, above all the desire to bind the
church to his person and Mission, will seem to com-
mend the wisdom of subsidy to the missionary whose
criterion is pragmatic. . . ." °

**Loss of
Popular
Appeal**

Second, the presentation of the indigenous church
to the home constituency involves the loss of a certain
popular financial appeal. The founding of the indigenous church is the primary objective of missionary
activity, and should therefore have the highest appeal
to well-informed Christians at home, yet it is a well-
known fact that many Christians respond more readily
in their missionary giving to an appeal for projects
which are really secondary. The plea to support an
orphan child, for example, or help famine suffers,
will bring a ready response. The visible often has more
appeal than the invisible, hence many missionaries
are tempted to carry on a type of work which makes
a better showing at home, and which brings in more
financial help.

Third, a sincere desire to show Christian charity
by helping the underprivileged and relieving suffering may cause the missionary to cling to procedures
that weaken the indigenous church.

**Honest
Christian
Charity**

The Bible inquires, "Whoso hath this world's good,
and seeth his brother have need, and shutteth up his
bowels of compassion from him, how dwelleth the
love of God in Him?" Then are not missionaries with
the resources of rich America behind them, obliged to
do everything in their power to relieve the want of the

° John Ritchie in *Indigenous Church Principles.*

less fortunate around them? Are we not to feed the hungry and clothe the naked for Christ's sake?

One of the factors which make the problem difficult to analyze is the difference in the standards of living. °"It is a recognized fact that there is a great contrast between the standard of living in the United States and most countries where foreign missionaries now work.... There is, therefore, the unconscious temptation on the part of the missionary to feel that he should try to raise the standard of living of the people to whom he ministers. The standard of living which he considers the norm is, of course, that of the United States of America. This is a false premise. Christian salvation is not a matter of civilization. It is true that backward civilizations have been greatly improved by the influence of the Lord Jesus Christ ... but this is a by-product of Christianity and is a historical result whenever Christ becomes an influence in the heart of individuals. This change in the standard of living, however, should come *through the national* church and not be imposed by foreign missionaries. Ideally, the only time financial assistance for an improved standard of living should be given to Christians in foreign lands is when the standard has been lowered *below normal* for that area by unusual circumstances (flood, famine, etc.)

"The gospel of salvation is effective in changing any people on any level of civilization. °° The duty of the missionary is not primarily to introduce higher standards of living ... (but) to preach the gospel and assist in building the church.... Satan is very eager

---

° This, and the following quotations in this chapter, unless otherwise credited, are taken, with slight adaptation, from a paper prepared by the Conservative Baptist Foreign Missions Society, *A Study of Indigenous Policies and Procedures.*

°°For further comment see *Salvation Independent of Economic Conditions,* World Dominion Movement, 156 Fifth Ave., New York.

to throw a smoke screen or fog around the whole missionary process in an effort to get the missionary and
the new Christians to dissipate their energies in an effort to change the physical aspects found in the mode
of living."

"The reason we are so interested in missions is not
only because Christ has commanded us to 'go into all
the world' but because we have realized the value of a
soul. We know it does *not* profit if a man gains the
whole world and loses his own soul. For this reason we
are interested in evangelism.... When, through the
Holy Spirit's leadership, this is accomplished, it not
only gives peace in the midst of existing conditions,
but often also gives an individual a desire to better his
social conditions. It would seem that those who hold
to indigenous principles are as much in favor of secur-
ing the social benefits of the gospel as any other
Christian group, with this modification: the supporters
of indigenous work believe that these benefits, the care
of the widows and orphans, the healing of the sick, the
education and training of the Christian constituency,
should come *through the church* instead of through the
missionary. Initial organizational plans and leadership may come from the missionary but ideally the
material support should come from the local church
and its environment. This is the indigenous method,
the New Testament way. To allow foreign material
resources to underwrite these features of the local
church program is to weaken the church. It will stunt
its growth.... Between those who can think and
work only for social betterment in foreign lands, and
those whose missionary work is only for the salvation
of souls, are those who have the concept of saving
souls in order that the national Christian church may
be established; which, in turn, will become the 'salt' of
the earth and implement the social blessings of the
Christian church. Anything that does not assist in
establishing the Church of Christ should be discour-

**Social
Benefits
Through
the Church**

aged. *Anything which hinders the development of the Church, no matter how much immediate good it does, should be sacrificed for the slower but more permanent good achieved through the establishment of the indigenous church.*

"By assisting the nationals to better their conditions with American funds and plans, there is always the danger of confusing the minds of the nationals as to what Christianity really is. In the minds of these Christians, the gospel message, with its emphasis on salvation, becomes mixed with the material by-products of the gospel. . . ."

It is quite apparent that whether it is in Africa, South America, or in Asia the people react in much the same way. They begin to expect material help wherever and whenever they can. . . . When we analyze the psychological results of free drugs, free schooling and free supplies upon the Christians, we soon find the "rice Christian" psychology manifesting itself. The people, being very human, naturally gravitate to the Mission where they can receive these material helps. When the material help is not forthcoming, then the individual missionary begins to sense a definite loss in their interest in his services. Some of these people being primitive are very frank and remark: 'What is the use of being a Christian if we do not receive these benefits?' It is then that we begin to realize that these things which we thought would help the people have only hindered and confused them. The gospel message and its intent have been confused with the benefits which we thought were so essential as an outward expression of our concept of the gospel. . . . The people have unconsciously joined the group who followed Jesus because they thought He would be King and provide them with food. . . . Eventually a clear thinking missionary begins to realize that these benefits must be foregone if he is to get the true message of salvation and

Confusing the Converts

Jesus' purpose in coming to this world across to these people who have lived in heathen darkness and idolatrous practices."

"Is there a place for social service by the missionary? Yes, as an individual but not as a missionary. As an individual, the missionary will always be helping in social service activities, donating money from his personal funds, ministering to the sick, etc., but he will refrain from using missions funds. He will, as a Christian, administer the cup of cold water in Christ's name but as a missionary he will concentrate his energy, time and foreign resources on the main task of planting the church."

Fourth the very ability and efficiency of the missionary may strangely enough prove to be a hindrance to the development of the church. Impatient to attain certain goals, the missionary may use the direct approach instead of the slower, indirect approach through the nationals. Americans are noted for their ability to get things done. We are psychologically geared to the machine age. *Fast* and *big* are words which occur frequently in our speech. "Within the boundaries of our evangelical standards, anything that will produce results more rapidly is looked upon with favor even though the permanent results may not be as satisfactory as (those) which might be obtained from other methods."

Want Quick Results

We Americans establish systems and a tempo that are beyond the capacity of the national. These do not fit his nature. He observes the way the missionary does things, and he knows that he cannot do them in that way, so he becomes discouraged. He cannot understand the American system of bookkeeping. He cannot carry through a complicated program that requires the coordination of several diverse activities. Again, the missionary may be a gifted musician and insist on the use of beautiful English hymns. Perhaps under his guidance, the converts learn to sing them with a piano accompaniment. When the missionary goes, the converts miss the piano, and their efforts to sing lack luster. Would it not be better to allow them to accompany their hymns on a one-stringed instrument with which they are familiar, one which they could continue to use when the missionary is not present?

Thus the missionary is sometimes too capable for the good of the national church. He does too much and sets too fast a pace. The converts watch him —not without admiration—and decide that since the missionary does things so well, he is the one to do them. Someone has illustrated this point by asking how we would feel if we were placed in the midst of a group of sleight-of-hand performers. Everything that we tried to do for ourselves, such as to dress ourselves, would be done for us by magic in the twinkling of an eye. Certainly we would end up feeling frustrated, bewildered, and discouraged, for we have not had training to fit us for that kind of life. Similarly the quick, efficient Americans are like sleight-of-hand performers to the slower nationals. It is futile to try to force them into our pattern. We only discourage them. Rather, the missionary is the one who needs to educate himself and change his ways so that he follows a pattern natural to the nationals. We should not make the pattern of the work so foreign that it requires a foreign education to carry it on.

The missionary for instance, may be unwilling to wait for a national church to find the resources and make the effort to put up its chapel. He knows that he can appeal to friends at home and receive more in one month than the church will raise in a year. His desire to "have something to show" for his labors may cause him to put to one side the efforts of the nationals and go ahead to put up the building with foreign funds.

Or, in a second instance, the missionary may feel that he should continue to fill the pastorate of the church where he resides, because there is no national worker "big enough" for the central church. Better crowds attend when the missionary preaches, and he is somewhat impatient with the slow and easy approach of the national workers. The trouble is that while there seem to be more immediate results through following nonindigenous practices, permanent results are far more discouraging. And permanent results, those which remain after the missionary has gone, are the true test of his labors.

RETHINK THIS CHAPTER

1. Discuss the conditions that result when a missionary is unwilling to surrender his authority.
2. Explain why some missionaries are tempted to follow nonindigenous methods.
3. Discuss how the honest desire of the missionary to show Christian charity may hinder him from attaining his true goal.
4. Explain how Christian charity on the part of the missionary has sometimes produced the "rice Christian" psychology in the nationals.
5. Since Christianity should bring social betterment, how can this be accomplished without weakening the moral fiber of the national converts?
6. Explain how the missionary's duty of social service may be carried on without hindering the establishing of the indigenous church.
7. How may the efficiency and ability of the missionary discourage national initiative?
8. How may the missionary's desire to see big results in a short time hinder the development of the indigenous church?

10

Relationship of the Missionary to
The Indigenous Church

The adjustment which the missionary is able to make to his environment and the relationship which he maintains with the church that he plants, have no small influence upon the success of his labors. In this chapter we shall discuss a few of the problems in this connection and then summarize the missionary's proper ministry.

The first problem is that of physical adjustment to the national environment, both in the home and in the general manner of life. Someone has stated that a missionary is "called to cross national and cultural barriers which separate the peoples of this world. He is the 'apostle to the Gentiles,' a calling which necessitates a break with his own people and the adoption of a new home in a strange land. But the mere fact that a person leaves his native land for a foreign shore is no indication that the national and cultural barrier has been crossed. The missionary frequently fails to make the break. He takes America with him. He establishes a small colony within the walls of the mission compound. . . . No effort is made to adopt the ways of the foreign country as we would expect a guest to adjust his life in the home of a friend." A consecrated Christian Indian worker makes this criticism: "It pains us to see that some of our excellent missionaries have so little appeal to the

Adjustment to Environment

121

people of India. This is because they live a life out of
all proportion to their environment. . . ."

Yet, we are here making no plea for the missionary
to "go native." We have observed that as a general
rule the nationals do expect the American missionary
to live on a different economic plane than the poorer
nationals can afford. As a matter of fact, whether the
national recognizes it or not, it would be almost a
physical impossibility for the missionary, with his wife
and children, to adjust to native food and housing
conditions. Even under the best conditions possible,
the missionaries suffer breakdowns in health because
of the diseases common to their new environment and
the changes in climate and food. The man of average
constitution finds it necessary either to live on a higher
scale than the nationals, or to discontinue missionary
work. Furthermore, it is only fair to the missionary's
children to rear them in an atmosphere that will
familiarize them a bit with American culture, so that
when they return to the homeland they will not be
misfits. These reasons are sufficient to explain the
necessity of a scale of living for the missionary that
would be beyond the reach of the average national.

Nevertheless, the missionary who lives in even the
most modest surroundings, according to American
standards, must seem, in the eyes of the nationals, to
live like a king. They cannot but know that the missionary family spends as much for one day's food as
the poor national will spend to feed an equal number
of people for nearly a week. And the missionary may
nonchalantly spend the equivalent of a day-laborer's
monthly wage for some item which appears to the
national to be a nonessential trinket. Thus missionaries, along with Americans in general, are considered "rich"; and it is useless for a missionary to
protest that he is poor, or that a ditchdigger in the
U.S. makes more money than he does.

This discrepancy is a source of vexation in the

mind of the national Christian and especially of the national worker, who struggles along with so little. It is also a source of distress to the conscientious missionary. Some such missionaries allow their sympathy to cloud their judgment. They begin to hand out financial gifts to the workers and Christians, thus starting down the road toward the very thing they desire to avoid: a church or worker financially dependent upon the Mission. The missionary should remember that with all of his struggles, the worker is doubtless no worse off financially than he was before his conversion. He is likely better off than his own brothers still in heathenism. On the other hand, the missionary should endeavor to live as simply as possible, and make no more show of money than is absolutely necessary. Explaining that articles of equipment such as his refrigerator and car were made possible by sacrificial gifts of friends who desired to help him and his family to live in a difficult climate and aid him in spreading the gospel, may help in giving the national the right perspective.

What about the use of modern transportation and equipment such as power saws, electric lights and public address systems? One Mission Board handles the question in this way: "Indigenous methods, strictly applied, would rule out these modern factors if they were beyond the mechanical and technological level of the people we are trying to reach. If nationals could not carry on with these modern things without the help of the white man, and if they could not afford to buy these things if they had to be replaced, then there is a doubt as to the advisability of their use. It can just as logically be argued that the using of these modern things increases the effectiveness of the missionary one thousand per cent. Both arguments are logical and right. This illustration may throw a bit of light on the problem: A good father can do a certain job better and faster than his son, but he lets his son

Modern Equipment

do it in order to teach him how to do it. He is preparing the son for the day when he will be on his
own. He will not train the son with tools which the
son himself cannot have later in life.

"From this illustration we may draw the general
conclusion which may answer both logical arguments
expressed above: As far as possible on compounds
and stations the missionary should use the transportation and mechanical developments used by the
people. This is one phase of 'reaching them on their
own level.' Where the missionary, after prayer and
consideration, feels that the advantages gained by
using modern things more than offset the disadvantages, he should use them only for personal use
and not try to integrate them into the indigenous
church. (Illustration: use a saw mill and a truck to
build, but do not give the saw and truck to the national church.) . . . Through all of this it should be kept
in mind that spiritual concepts taught (and ab-
sorbed) are far more important and lasting than any
material progress made. . . . Even though the nationals may greatly desire the foreign aid, we must
carefully evaluate whether or not it will weaken the
recipients." °

A second problem, the financial relationships of
the missionary with the indigenous church and the
danger of the wrong use of foreign funds, has already
been mentioned. What is the legitimate use of foreign funds in missionary work, outside of the personal
support and expenses of the missionary himself?

"Of course missionaries and Missions should not
be niggardly. There is a wise and loving use of money
which opens the very gates of heaven to many a soul.
But on mission fields, as at home, it is easy to . . .

° From *A Study of Indigenous Policies and Procedures*, prepared by the Conservative Baptist Foreign Missions Society.

(misinterpret) a warm, sacrificial love of Christ and love for the people which would pour itself out for them without thought of remuneration, . . . (and respond with) a calculating, selfish attitude which demands so much pay for so much work. Indeed, every missionary society at home ought to make sure that its money is not used to the detriment of that which it would build up.

"Although a missionary must be extremely careful in the use of money, nevertheless he must show the people that it has cost him something to bring the gospel to them. Financial gifts rarely impress native Christians as involving any real sacrifice. On many fields the people in general think that all foreigners, Americans especially, are rich, and Christians share these views. It is in this connection that actual physical hardship and suffering speak to foreign peoples more eloquently than does the sacrifice of position, loved ones or native land. Indeed, I have seen a pair of blistered feet do more for the advancement of the gospel than had gifts of hundreds of dollars by the missionary who owned those feet.

"This principle carries all the way through. Though one may deny a plea for funds with which to build a church, if he will sit down and help a congregation to figure out ways and means of building that church, if he will help them with his own hands, the people will see that he is actually giving in a way that costs. *To sum it up, one might say that the missionary should do only those things which the young church is unable to do for itself, not the things it is unwilling to do. And he should make certain that he does not decide too quickly, too unwisely, that a church is actually unable to do any task whatever that faces it."* °

Limited Use of Foreign Funds

As a general policy, foreign funds may best be

° The Independent Board Bulletin.

invested in those aspects of the work that are beyond the reach of the local churches, that serve to advance the work in the *district,* rather than the local church. Such use of foreign money can be a blessing *as long as we do not build in dependence upon those funds, nor substitute the effort of the nationals with that of our own,* and so cripple initiative. We are to help the churches do things, not do things for them.

A project which would hasten the evangelization of a new district, could well merit the wise investment of foreign funds. In my opinion, a Bible school for the training of national workers is one project where foreign funds may really be of help. Yet those funds should not be used in such a way as to cause the student and churches to expect the Mission to carry the financial burden for them. Investment in a tract of land in order to raise food for the Bible school, under the supervision of the national church, could well pay rich, dividends, and help to make the Bible school self-supporting. Always the missionary must think in terms of a self-supporting work. He should initiate each department of the work in such a manner that the nationals can carry on after he has gone. He should refrain from starting anything that the nationals themselves cannot maintain after the withdrawal of the missionary and his funds.

It is now in order that we should summarize the missionary's *ministry* to the indigenous church:

Missionary's Ministry Summarized

a. The missionary is primarily a planter of churches. This work includes two phases: evangelizing the unconverted, and teaching the converts, which in turn, includes the training of national workers and leaders.

b. The missionary is a temporary factor in any local area, and he should build the church in such a way that it will be able to continue after he has gone. He should not center the work in himself or in the Mission, but make the church the center.

c. Since the missionary is a temporary factor, he

should not allow himself to become bogged down with the routine of maintaining the work, but seek to occupy new fields. He cannot expect every detail of evangelism and organization to be worked out perfectly before he relinquishes the direct oversight.

d. If the missionary finds an indigenous work already under way in his area, either the product of spontaneous national effort, or the fruit of missionary labors, he must be extremely careful not to adopt measures that will choke it out. Missionaries are usually eager to get such works "in hand" (which means, under Mission control), and in doing so they can easily stifle them. The missionary may be tempted to pay a salary to the leader of the indigenous work. Later he may find the converts doing only a small part, with pay, in comparison to what they previously did without his financial assistance.

e. The missionary should refuse to occupy a position that a national can fill. He should avoid becoming tied down to a local pastorate, but keep free for the work of extension. He should count it a triumph when he is able to place upon the shoulders of national leaders the responsibilities which he has been carrying.

f. The missionary should not be jealous of his own authority or position, but be willing for others to take the lead. He should earn his position of leadership in the national church on the merits of his character and ministry. He must not feel that he merits a position of authority because he is a missionary. If the national church has produced leaders who can fill the offices in the work, the missionary should not object to their taking office; nay, he should insist that they do so. The missionary's spiritual ministry will always provide him his proper place in the Body of Christ, whether he holds an office or not.

g. There is undoubtedly a danger that the missionary may withdraw too soon from the work. But

**Time of
Withdrawal**

there is also the danger that he may fail to withdraw at the proper time. A withdrawal is premature
when a missionary leaves the field before he has
provided for the teaching and leadership that are
vital to the indigenous church. A church left without
leaders and teachers is subject to the dangers of
error and fanaticism. Converts may lapse back into
heathenism and the church disintegrate. These dangers can be avoided by following the Pauline example. He did not leave the churches he founded
without instruction or leadership. Thus, it is not
enough that the missionary gather a group of converts; they must be incorporated into a church under
the guidance of the Holy Spirit.

Failure to withdraw at the proper time breeds
discontent and dwarfs the national Christian leadership. It also holds the missionary in that one district when he could move on to a fruitful pioneer
ministry.

After the missionary has turned over the leadership of the national church to its own leaders, he may
still serve that church by placing himself at its disposal. He may be asked to help in the Bible school
with the training of national workers; or it may be
desired that he push an aggressive evangelization
program in some unevangelized area of the district.
At the same time he will strengthen the new administration with his counsel. When a national leadership has been developed sufficient to guide the
churches; when there are national brethren prepared
to teach new workers in the Bible school; and when a
progressive evangelism has been initiated in the main
areas of the district; then the missionary's work in that
district is finished. He can with a grateful heart move
on into a neighboring district, or transfer to a new
field, to begin once more his unique ministry as a
planter of churches.

In no other aspect will the missionary influence

the indigenous church as he will in the matter of spiritual leadership. Above everything else, he must be a spiritual example to his converts and to the workers, a man who can prevail with God and prepare the way for the moving of the Holy Spirit. It is sad, then, when national converts and Christians outstrip the missionary in spiritual vision. They look to the missionary not merely for his organizational ability and Bible knowledge, but for leadership and inspiration. Sometimes they have not found these qualities in the missionary and have had to go on without him. Above all else, let the missionary maintain his standing as a "man of God." With this relationship maintained, all other relationships will be made easy.

The Missionary's Spiritual Leadership

RETHINK THIS CHAPTER

1. Explain the problem that faces the missionary in adjusting to the national environment.
2. Discuss the question as to whether or not a missionary should "go native" in order to win the people.
3. Why is the ordinary American considered "rich" by the nationals?
4. What argument can be presented in favor of using modern equipment?
5. What argument can be presented against the use of modern equipment?
6. What policy should guide the missionary in his decision as to whether he will use modern equipment or not?
7. Explain how a missionary may help the national church without making a financial gift.
8. If foreign funds are available to help the work on a certain field, where can they best be employed? Illustrate.
9. Discuss the tendency of the missionary to sacrifice mobility for the sake of maintaining an established work.
10. Discuss the temptation that besets the missionary when he finds a spontaneous effort under way in his area.
11. Explain the attitude which the missionary should take concerning his own ministry, and the occupying of official posts in the national church.

12. Discuss the danger of withdrawing prematurely from the national church.
13. What are the dangers which confront the missionary and the church if the missionary delays his withdrawal too long?
14. When may a missionary safely consider that his work is done in a given district?
15. In what way may a missionary make the greatest impression for good upon the national church?

11

Pentecost and Indigenous Methods

Spiritual awakenings and revivals can be lost through lack of proper methods for harnessing these movements and conserving their results. This is one reason why indigenous methods are so important. A great revival can die out or become ineffective if it is not channeled in a scriptural course toward New Testament goals. Furthermore, even the best methods will produce nothing unless accompanied by the work of the Holy Spirit. What gasoline and spark are to the mechanism of a well-tuned motor, spiritual power is to indigenous church methods, for two essential factors combine to make the church a going concern. The mechanics of a successful church on the mission field are the New Testament methods: the dynamics are the power and ministries of the Holy Spirit. Either factor alone is incomplete and inadequate.

This perhaps explains why we have reports from some sections that indigenous methods have been tried, but that after reaching a certain stage, the work failed to make progress. The workers, they say, lacked initiative and the churches barely held their own. Some have used this as an argument against the indigenous method. They claim that the nationals simply are not up to an aggressive program; that left to themselves they lapse into inertia; and that a missionary must constantly be on hand to inspire and direct if the church is to make progress. The trouble will not be found in the indigenous methods, for these are the New Testament methods. The difficulty may be that the indigenous methods have been *only partially or imperfectly applied;* or on the other hand, having been applied, *they have not been accompanied by New Testament power.* New Testament Christians received such an enduement of power, such an inflow of divine life, that their doubts, fears and inertia were swept aside. They "went everywhere" testifying of the resurrection of Christ. Though we may have perfectly set up the "mechanism" of an indigenous church, if it lacks the divine "combustible" of the Holy Spirit's power, it will still be ineffective.

The genius of the Pentecostal movement is uniquely suited to the indigenous church method. We have witnessed thousands of "indigenous" churches spring into existence in the homeland as a result of Pentecostal outpourings since the turn of the century. Pentecostal outpourings, whether in the homeland or abroad, have always produced converts with flaming zeal and sacrificial spirit.

On the mission field, the emphasis which Pentecostal people place on the necessity of each individual believer receiving a personal infilling of the Holy Spirit has produced believers and workers of unusual **Pentecost** zeal and power. Again, the emphasis on the present-**Uniquely** day working of miracles and the healing of the sick has **Suited** been the means in the hand of God of awakening whole communities and convincing unbelievers of the power of God. These have seen a Power at work superior to that of their own witch doctors and priests. The faith which Pentecostal people have in the ability of the Holy Spirit to give spiritual gifts and supernatural abilities to the common people, even to those who might be termed "ignorant and unlearned," has raised up a host of lay preachers and leaders of unusual spiritual ability—not unlike the rugged fishermen who first followed the Lord.

We have witnessed the miracle of transformation which the presence of the Holy Spirit produces in a national church. We have seen lethargic and reluctant workers transformed into zealous witnesses, willing to launch out into new towns and villages without any promise of support. Suspicious, sensitive, and squabbling believers have been melted together by divine love and have become a powerful force for the kingdom of God.

It was a vital turning point in one Central American field, when seventy-five believers were filled with the Spirit in one week. This number included several workers. In the following eighteen months, about three hundred received the fulness of the Spirit, and within two years from the first blessing, the number of workers had practically doubled. So had the number of churches and converts. Within a few months, the gospel was preached in sections of the country far interior, where under ordinary circumstances it would not have penetrated for many years.

To be successful in the indigenous church ministry, the missionary must not only be able to teach and initiate the converts in right methods, but also be able to introduce them into the realm of the Holy Spirit's workings. New Testament methods coupled with New Testament power is the answer to the present-day problems of our mission fields. Let the missionaries of each field gather together to pray until there comes from heaven the spiritual power necessary for an awakening according to the apostolic pattern. Let them initiate the converts also into this prayer ministry for revival. Let missionaries and nationals not only preach a gospel of power, but pray until they themselves catch the flame in their own hearts. It is impossible to expend more energy than we receive from our Source. We must give time, both individually and collectively, to this most important of all ministries.

Producing the Power

To pray until God's blessings are poured out upon the district of his labors, to channel those blessings by New Testament methods toward the founding of a vigorous national church—this is the ministry which justifies the presence of the missionary on the foreign soil and gives him a rightful claim to the noble title of "Church Builder."

o   o   o   o   o

JESUS SAID: "I WILL BUILD MY CHURCH; AND THE GATES OF HELL SHALL NOT PREVAIL AGAINST IT."

"AND THEY WENT FORTH, AND PREACHED EVERY WHERE, THE LORD WORKING WITH THEM, AND CONFIRMING THE WORD WITH SIGNS FOLLOWING."

RETHINK THIS CHAPTER

1. Distinguish between the mechanics and dynamics of the indigenous church.
2. Why have indigenous methods failed in some areas? Give two reasons.
3. Discuss the statement that the "genius of the Pentecostal movement is uniquely suited to the indigenous church method."
4. How do the Pentecostal teachings on (a) the baptism in the Holy Spirit, (b) divine healing, and (c) the gifts of the Spirit contribute to the development of the indigenous church?
5. What steps should be taken by the missionary to bring the divine power of the Holy Spirit into operation in the national church?

Appendix A.

Suggested Policy for Missionary Work°

1. *Objective.*

The winning of souls to Christ and establishing of assemblies in all places where converts are won, should be regarded as the primary objective of all missions. All other branches of ministry should be subordinated to this.

2. *The Local Assembly.*

A. We recognize the local assembly as God's agency through which the Holy Spirit works for the edification of believers and the evangelization of the surrounding regions.

B. We recognize the local assembly as entitled to self-government under Jesus Christ, its living Head, and as having the right to administer discipline to its members in accordance with the Scriptures and under the guidance of the Holy Spirit.

C. The spiritual leadership in the local assembly is not necessarily a paid pastor, and where there is no pastor, leadership may be exercised by elders and deacons who are self-supporting.

D. Every assembly should be a training center for instruction in the Word of God and in spiritual ministry.

E. Every assembly established should be self-

° From the Missionary Manual of the Foreign Missions Department of the General Council of the Assemblies of God.

supporting from the beginning, although in some places where property is expensive and preaching places can be secured only at considerable expenditures, this principle may have to be modified for a time.

3. *The Missionary.*

A. The ministry of the missionary is one of great importance, since he is an ambassador for Christ and is sent as God's representative to the people. He must remember that above all else he is a servant, and should never consider that race or control of finances entitle him to exercise lordship over the assemblies. As soon as the national converts manifest gifts of ministry they should be encouraged to take responsibility.

B. The missionary should never consider that he is permanent in any one place, but ever have his eyes on the regions beyond, seeking to make the assembly in each place a self-supporting and self-propagating unit. He will, of course, like the apostle Paul, find it necessary to exercise a spiritual oversight over the new assemblies until they are fully established, after which a Council should be formed by the local assemblies to supervise their own work.

C. Great care should be exercised in the purchase or erection of buildings. Wherever possible church buildings should be erected by the nationals. Missionary residences, rest homes, and Bible schools may have to be financed from home sources.

D. Missionary policy and program for the development of the field shall be governed by the indigenous church principles as set forth by the General Council. No project shall be undertaken that eventually cannot be taken over, supported and managed by the national church. While precedence in the work and the practices of other mission societies should be carefully considered, these are not to be accepted as guides. However, when methods have already been introduced which are not in harmony with indigenous principles, patience, wisdom, and tact are required in establishing a new policy to avoid disrupting the harmony and unity of the work. Such changes may require years to work out.

4. *The Bible School.*

A. The Bible school is necessary to give more advanced training to men and women who have proved themselves in their local assemblies as having a call from God for special service.

B. In every Bible school the ordinary standards of native life in that country should be observed in order not to alienate the students from their own people.

Appendix B

Suggested Guide for the Instruction of New Converts

Reference has been made in Chapter III, "Self-Government," to the standard of membership for local assemblies, adopted by the Assemblies of God in Central America. ° The following is a translation from Spanish of this standard. It is given here as an illustration and suggested guide for other fields where something similar may be needed. This booklet was prepared especially for new converts, the greater part of whom came out of Roman Catholicism. For that reason those doctrinal truths are presented first which will help clarify certain unscriptural ideas generally held by the people. Naturally, in a non-Catholic area, a different order may be preferable.

To conserve space, this "Standard" has been slightly abridged here. Questions to aid in the study of each section have been deleted.

° Ralph D. Williams and Francisco R. Arbizu originally prepared the "Standard" for the work in El Salvador, Central America.

STANDARD OF FAITH AND FELLOWSHIP
for the
Local Assemblies of God in Central America

PROLOGUE

The purpose of this booklet is to set forth essential
Biblical doctrines and practices as a basis of faith and
fellowship among the members of the local church.
These doctrines are phrased so that they may be easily
taught to the new convert and readily understood by
him. Moreover, the booklet will explain to the convert the new relationships which he now enjoys with
other believers, and will teach him how to behave
worthily as a member of the church to which he is to
belong.

The pastor, or someone designated by him, will hold
weekly classes for new converts during two or three
months, until he has finished teaching this booklet.
Those who attend these classes are called "members
under instruction." At the end of this time of instruction, those who have studied will be examined as
to their faithfulness to Christ and their comprehension
of Christian truth. Having given satisfactory evidence
of their Christian life to the Official Board of the
church, they shall be baptized in water and become
"active members."

In case sufficient proof of the sincerity of any
member under instruction is lacking, he will not be
baptized, but his case will be considered again at the
time of the next baptizing.

The Bible ordains the teaching of Christian doctrine

1. The disciples were sent to teach in all the world.
Matth. 28:19, 20; Mark 16:15.

2. After Pentecost, the apostles taught the truths
of the gospel both to converted and unconverted.
Acts 2:40-42; 11:26; 19:9,10; 20:20; and 2 Tim. 2:1,2.

3. Believers in Jesus Christ who obey the Word
of God will receive the following benefits:

a. They will have a firm foundation for their faith and a guide to help them in the service of God. 2 Tim. 3:16, 17.

b. They are promised the continual presence of Christ with them, who will confirm His Word with signs following. Matt. 20:20; Mark 16:20.

c. They will partake of the love of God. Jn. 14:15, 21, 24; 15:10.

d. They will enjoy true spiritual liberty. Jn. 8:31, 32; Rom. 8:1,2.

I. THE PURPOSE OF THE LOCAL CHURCH

Believers in Christ who live in the same community should gather together to form a local church or assembly. Matt. 18:17, 20; Acts 8:1, and 9:31. The purpose of this assembly is:

1. To worship God in spirit and in truth. Jn. 4:23, 24; Psa. 117; Col. 3:16. This is our spiritual worship.

2. To be instructed in the holy doctrines of the Scriptures, and so grow in knowledge, holiness, and love. 2 Pet. 3:18; 2 Tim. 3:14-17; Psa. 119:9; 2 Cor. 7:1; Jn. 13:34. This is our education and culture.

3. To spread the knowledge of the gospel everywhere, by means of the testimony of a good life and by preaching the Word of God. Mark 16:15; Acts 1:8. This is our service to humanity.

II. FUNDAMENTAL DOCTRINES

A. *The Church of Christ*

1. The Church of Christ is a people (a) redeemed by the blood of Jesus (Eph. 1:7); (b) separated from the world (2 Cor. 6:16-18); (c) believing the gospel (Jn. 20:31); and (d) fulfilling the Christian precepts (Titus 2:11-14).

2. The spiritual nature of the Church is revealed by the following symbols:

a. The body of Christ. Eph. 1:22; 5:23; 1 Cor. 12:12,

27. This symbol reveals the spiritual relation that exists between Christ and the believer, as well as the union among believers. It also shows that the spiritual authority rests in Christ, the head, and not in any intermediate person on the earth. Nevertheless the ministry of the gospel is carried on by men. Eph. 4:11-16.

b. A building or temple. 1 Cor. 3:9, 16; 1 Pet. 2:6, 7; Eph. 2:20-22. The believers are the "spiritual stones" used in the construction of this spiritual temple. This establishes first of all that Christ is the Rock upon which the Church is founded and second, that it is an error to teach that the Church is founded on Saint Peter, since he was only one of the apostles, and as an apostle, was a part of the foundation as were all the others. Eph. 2:20. This teaches that God dwells in the Church to guide and bless her.

c. The True Vine. Jn. 15:1, 2. Christ and the believer are united in the same spiritual life as the branch receives its life from the vine. The believer is a branch that ought to bear fruit. God, the Husbandman, purges each believer so that he will bear more fruit. Heb. 12:5, 6-11. This symbol teaches us that the believer is made partaker of the divine nature which imparts to him faith, grace, love, and courage; second, that the believer should bear fruit, bringing other souls to Christ; and third, that God disciplines His sons so that they will walk in holiness and be fruitful in service.

3. How to become a member of the Church. The all-important requirement in order to be a member of the Church of Christ is regeneration. Jn. 3:3-5. Three steps are necessary:

a. Faith in Christ and in His blood that cleanses from sin. Jn. 14:6; 3:6, 16; Acts 16:31; Eph. 1:7; 1 Jn. 1:7, 9.

b. True repentance. Acts 2:38; Matt. 9:13. This means to confess our sins to God and to forsake them. 1 Jn. 1:9; Jn. 8:11; 5:14; Prov. 28:13.

c. A public confession of faith in Christ. Rom. 10:9, 10; Mark 8:38.

4. The work of the Church in the earth.

a. To preach to every creature. Matt. 28:19; 1 Pet. 2:9, 10.

b. To maintain the Bible standard of holiness and righteousness before the world. Eph. 5:25-27; Matt. 5:13-16.

c. ° To be zealous of good works. Titus 2:14; Gal. 6:10; Matt. 5:16, 44, 45.

5. The financial support of the Church in the earth. Salvation cannot be purchased with money, nor can we pay for the spiritual blessings God sends us. Isa. 55:1, 2; Matt. 10:8. Funds are required to pay the expenses of the ministry and evangelize the world. The Church is supported financially by its members. This is natural, for the members are those who have the greatest interest in the Church's mission. The tenth part of the believer's income is the portion which should be dedicated to the work of God. This is the tithe. Offerings are gifts over and above the tithes. Tithing for the work of God has ever been the practice of faithful men of God in the three principal periods of Bible History.

a. *In the period of the patriarchs,* centuries before Moses gave the Law, men of God paid tithes. Gen. 14:18-20; Heb. 7:4; Gen. 28:22.

b. *Under the Law of Moses,* tithing was established. Lev. 27:30-34. It was of such importance that God pronounced special blessings on those who fulfilled this requirement and cursings upon those who failed to do so. Mal. 3:8-10.

c. *The period of the Church.* Although the Church is not under the Law of Moses (Luke 16:16; Rom.

° Point "c," while not included in the original booklet, has been added here at the suggestion of Foreign Missions Department officials.

6:14), yet St. Paul referred to the system of tithing under the Law as a model for the support of the ministry. Num. 18:21 and 1 Cor. 9:13, 14. Note the words "even so" of verse 14. (See also the words of Jesus in Matt. 23:23.)

It is important to note the difference between the system of tithing under the Law and as it is practiced by the Church. The Israelites did it by obligation under the Law, while believers give from love and gratitude to God. 2 Cor. 9:6-8. The entire chapter 8 of Second Corinthians deals with the grace of liberality. Verse 2 shows that poverty and tribulation make our gift greater in the eyes of God. Verse 7 teaches that we should not desire gifts and graces of the Holy Spirit while neglecting the grace of liberality.

B. The Holy Bible

1. The Bible is the inspired Word of God by which He reveals His will to His people. 2 Peter 1:20, 21. It is the infallible rule of faith and conduct to guide us from earth to glory. Psa. 119:11, 105; Jn. 5:24; 20:31.°

2. We should not add to, nor take away from the Bible. 1 Peter 1:25; Rev. 22:18, 19.

C. The One True God

The one true God has revealed Himself as the Eternal "I AM"; and further has revealed that He exists as a Holy Trinity: as Father, Son and Holy Ghost. Deut. 6:4; Mark 12:29; Isa. 43:10, 11; Matt. 28:19; 2 Cor. 13:14.

D. The Salvation of the Soul

1. The salvation of the soul is a spiritual and miraculous transformation which God effects in the individual who exercises faith in the Word of God,

---

° Explanation might well be added here to the effect that the rules that govern a Christian's conduct are to be found particularly in the New Testament, rather than in the Old. See Matt. 5:27, 28, 38, 39. (MLH.)

faith in the blood of Jesus, and repents of his sin. Jn. 3:3-5; 2 Cor. 5:17; Jn. 1:11-13; 1 Peter 1:18, 19, 23; Acts 2:38.

2. Only in Christ is there salvation. Acts 4:10-12; 16:30, 31; Jn. 14:6; 1 Tim. 2:5. There is no salvation through the Law of Moses (Rom. 3:20-22); nor through the worship of images (Ex. 20:4, 5; Isa. 44:9-18). Mary, the mother of our Lord, is not able to save us—rather she too, needed a Saviour. Acts 4:12; Luke 1:46-48.

E. A Holy Life—Sanctification

God is holy, and requires that His children be holy. 1 Peter 1:15, 16; Heb. 12:14.

1. Sanctification means (a) cleansing from sin; (b) separation from sin and; (c) consecration to God. 2 Chron. 29:5, 15; 1 Thess. 4:3; 2 Cor. 6:17; Num. 8:17.

2. Sanctification is attained through (a) faith in the Word (Jn. 17:17; Eph. 5:26); (b) faith in the blood of Jesus (Heb. 10:10, 29); and (c) the work of the Holy Spirit in our lives (1 Pet. 1:2; Gal. 5:5, 16, 22).

3. Sanctification is effected (a) instantaneously, at the time of conversion (1 Cor. 6:10, 11); and (b) continuously, each day as the believer walks with God (2 Cor. 7:1; 1 Jn. 1:7).

F. Prayer

Prayer is the privilege and duty of every person. 1 Tim. 2:8. It is a drawing near to God in spiritual communion in order to worship Him and praise Him for His mercies (Psa. 103:1; Phil. 4:6); to bring our requests to Him (1 Jn. 5:14; Jn. 15:7; Matt. 7:7); and to intercede on behalf of others (Eph. 3:14-17; 1 Sam. 12:23). Prayer should be made to God in the name of Jesus Christ (Jn. 14:13, 14); in the power of the Holy Spirit (Eph. 6:18; Rom. 8:26); and with understanding (1 Cor. 14:15).

G. The baptism in the Holy Spirit.

1. The baptism in the Holy Spirit was not only for

the apostles but is the privilege of every converted person. Acts 2:38, 39; Matt. 3:11.

2. Each believer should seek with faith until he receives. Luke 24:49; Acts 1:4, 5.

3. The baptism in the Holy Spirit is accompanied by the initial evidence of speaking in other tongues as the Spirit gives utterance. Acts 2:4; 10:44, 46; 19:6; Mark 16:17-20.

4. The baptism in the Spirit gives power to be a faithful witness. Acts 1:8; 4:31.

H. *Divine Healing*

1. Divine healing is promised in the Holy Scriptures. Mark 16:18; James 5:14, 15.

2. Healing from sickness has been provided in the atonement, along with salvation from sin. Healing is the privilege of every believer. Isa. 53:4, 5; 1 Pet. 2:24.

3. Christ healed all who came to Him. Matt. 8:16, 17.

4. God is our healer. Ex. 15:26.

I. *The Future Return of Christ*

The second coming of Christ is the blessed hope of the believer.

1. At the time of His coming the Church will be caught up to meet Him, including both those who have died in Christ, and those who are still alive. 1 Thess. 4:16, 17.

2. After this extraordinary happening, the Lord will come to the earth with His holy saints, bringing salvation to His people, Israel, and will reign upon the earth for a thousand years. Rev. 20:4.

J. *Eternal Condemnation*

After the millennium, the wicked dead will be raised and made to appear before the great white throne where they will be judged according to their works and then cast into the lake of fire. Rev. 20:11-15; Matt. 25:41.

III. SACRAMENTS

A. *Christian Baptism*

1. Christian baptism is a type of our death to the "old man" and the resurrection of the "new man" to walk in "newness of life." Rom. 6:4; Eph. 4:22-24.

2. Baptism is a testimony of faith in Jesus Christ. Therefore the sincerity of the faith of the candidate should be clearly manifest. 1 Pet. 3:21; Acts 8:26-38; Col. 2:12. This explains why it is not possible to baptize infants: they cannot give a testimony of faith.

3. Baptism is administered in the name of the Father, and of the Son, and of the Holy Ghost. Matt. 28:19.

4. The word "baptize" in the original Scriptures signifies "to immerse." This harmonizes with the teaching of Rom. 6:3, 4.

B. *The Lord's Supper*

1. This sacrament was instituted by the Lord who commanded that it should be practiced until His second coming. Matt. 26:26-30; 1 Cor. 11:23-31.

2. The bread and the wine represent the body and blood of Christ. His body was broken when He carried our sins on the cross. His blood establishes the New Covenant. 1 Cor. 11:24, 25.

3. The Lord's Supper is observed in memory of the death of Jesus and contains a promise of His second coming. 1 Cor. 11:26.

4. It is the privilege and duty of every active member to participate in the Lord's Supper, for it is a symbol of our partaking of the divine nature. Jn. 6:53.

5. It is necessary that the believer examine himself first, so as not to take the Lord's Supper unworthily. 1 Cor. 11:28. (Note: If a believer feels that he is spiritually unprepared to partake, instead of refusing to do so, he should seek God for pardon and renew his consecration to God, and thus he will be

able to partake with all the church. In this way the Lord's Supper will be a means of keeping the spiritual life of the church at a high level.)

(Here follows an explanation of the ceremonies of the dedication of Children, the Marriage Ceremony and the Funeral Service, which are not included here for lack of space.)

IV. THE MEMBERS OF THE CHURCH

A. *Requirements for Membership.* The member must:

1. Have experienced salvation through faith in Christ, and have expressed his desire to follow Him all the days of his life. Rom. 10:9, 10.

2. If married, have been married according to civil law. 1 Cor. 6:9; 7:2, 10, 11; 1 Pet. 2:13; Heb. 13:4.

3. Have studied this Standard of Faith and Fellowship carefully and have agreed to fulfil its teachings.

4. Have been baptized in water. Matt. 28:19; Acts 2:38.

(Note: A believer may also be received by letter of recommendation from the Official Board of another Assembly of our fellowship. When a believer does not present a letter of recommendation, he should be received as an "inactive" member until information can be obtained concerning his conduct.)

B. *Duties of Members*

1. To live a consecrated life and not contaminate oneself with the world. 2 Peter 1:4-8; 1 Cor. 6:9-11.

2. To learn how to win souls for Christ. Acts 8:4.

3. To honor, respect and support the pastor. 1 Thess. 5:12, 13; Heb. 13:17; 1 Cor. 9:12-14.

4. To contribute to the support of the work with tithes and offerings. Mal. 3:10; Matt. 23:23.

5. To attend regularly the services of the church.

6. To dedicate Sunday to the service of the Lord. Acts 20:7.

7. To establish a family altar in the home, as conditions permit.

8. To vote in the business sessions of the church, seeking God's guidance for every decision.

C. The Privileges of Members

1. To receive the ministry of the Word from the pastor. Acts 20:27, 28.

2. To receive visits from the pastor.

3. To take part in the activities of the church.

4. To receive the Lord's Supper.

5. A member may be named to fill one of the official posts in the church.

6. A member may receive license as a lay preacher to help in the work in the outstations.

7. Each member shall receive a membership card.

D. The Member's Responsibility to Other Members

1. To visit the sick, help the needy, comfort those in trouble, and strive to maintain harmonious relationships with all. 1 Thess. 5:14; Heb. 12:14; James 1:27; Matt. 25:35-40.

2. To pray for a brother overtaken in a fault. 1 Jn. 5:16.

3. To withdraw from those who cause divisions. Rom. 16:17; 2 Thess. 3:6, 7, 13-16.

E. The Member's Responsibility Toward the Unconverted

1. To live a clean life and give a good testimony of the power and grace of God. 1 Pet. 2:9, 12, 15; 1 Thess. 5:22; Matt. 5:13-16.

2. To strive to give the gospel to the unsaved and pray for their salvation. 2 Cor. 5:18, 19; 1 Tim. 2:1-7.

3. To love his enemies. Matt. 5:43-48.

V. DISCIPLINE

When a member is accused of a fault of such a nature that it affects the testimony and standard which the church is endeavoring to maintain, that member should be called before the Committee in charge of discipline. (The Committee shall be composed of the members of the Official Board. If the case so requires, one or two other members of the church may be added to the Committee. Matt. 18:15; 1 Cor. 6:1-5).

The purpose of this Committee is:

1. To correct the fault. 2 Cor. 7:8, 9.

2. To restore the offender. Gal. 6:1; Matt. 6:14, 15.

3. To preserve the good testimony of the church. 1 Tim. 3:7; Titus 1:10-13.

4. To protect other members from falling into the same error. 1 Cor. 5:6, 7.

The Committee shall proceed in the following manner:

1. The Committee shall meet, and the accused shall be called in. This should be done as soon as possible after the fault has become known.

2. In case the accused denies his guilt, he must not be judged guilty unless his guilt is proved by trustworthy witnesses. 2 Cor. 13:1.

3. If when the accused person is called before the Committee, he does not wish to appear, then he shall be judged after the testimony of the witnesses has been heard. 1 Cor. 5:3,4.

4. The Committee shall endeavor to arrive at the real truth in the case, and if the accused is found guilty, the Committee should endeavor with love to lead him to a sincere repentance in order that he may be restored. 2 Cor. 2:7, 8.

5. If the accused humbles himself in true repentance, asking pardon of the church in public, he shall be pardoned. Matt. 6:14, 15.

6. Disciplinary action should not be considered as a punishment. A time of discipline, determined according to the seriousness of his sin, shall be decided upon

for the fallen brother who desires to be restored; first, as a measure to prove the sincerity of his repentance; and second, to give time for the other members to observe his genuine restoration before he is permitted to exercise all of his privileges as a member of the church.

7. During the time when a member is under discipline, he shall not exercise the usual privileges of membership;° however, he must be faithful in attending the services. The time of discipline may be from one to three months, not more than this period except in very exceptional cases.

8. The recommendation of the Committee shall be made public in the next meeting of the church, for its approval.

9. If the offender does not manifest a spirit of humility and repentance, this shall be sufficient reason to remove his name from the list of members. 1 Cor. 5:13.

10. When such a person has been removed from the list and desires to be readmitted, he should present his

---

° See "Privileges of Members," 3, 4, 5, and 6. It has been objected that since partaking of the Lord's Supper is a means of grace, this privilege should not be denied to a member under discipline. The writer, also, was reluctant at first to accept the position of the national brethren in this regard. However, in a Roman Catholic community, Holy Communion is given to a communicant only after he has gone to confession and done penance. Hence, in the public mind, it is a symbol of full restoration. Our Central American brethren feel that much damage is done to the testimony of the church when a member guilty of a grievous sin, such as drunkenness or immorality, is permitted to partake of the Lord's Supper before he has given proof of the sincerity of his repentance. Such a one may soon after repeat his fault, and then again ask forgiveness. This is precisely the common practice among Catholics in that area. It is felt that to permit such an unhappy situation in our own assemblies would do more harm to the sinning individual and to the church than would result by depriving him of the privilege of partaking of the Lord's Supper for a brief time, while he proved the sincerity of his repentance.

This is presented as an example of how an indigenous church may solve its own problems. It is not insisted upon as a guide for other fields. MLH.

petition in writing to the Official Board of the church.

11. A member who intentionally stays away from services for six months, and who also withdraws his support shall be liable to the cancellation of his membership.

VI. THE OFFICIAL BOARD

The Official Board shall work for the smooth functioning of all the activities of the church and for its spiritual development. It also shall be responsible for the providing of a place of worship and the necessary equipment. Acts 6:3; Tit. 1:5.

1. The members of the Official Board shall be the pastor and from three to seven deacons, depending on the size of the assembly. These members shall name a secretary and a treasurer from among themselves. The pastor is president of all the sessions of the Official Board and of the church, except the annual sessions in which the pastor is elected, in which case he shall turn over the chair to the first deacon, or to one of the presbyters or executive officers of the Conference, if present.

2. The pastor shall be elected, or reelected, each year. This applies also to the rest of the members of the Official Board.

3. The deacons should be men of spiritual fitness and consecration, having been active members of the church for at least one year. 1 Tim. 3:8-13.

4. The duties of the Official Board.

a. The pastor is responsible for the faithful ministry of the Word of God in the services and has the general direction of the activities of the church.

b. The deacons are to help the pastor in the activities of the church as follows:

(1) Visitation.

(2) Forming part of the Committee in charge of discipline.

(3) Seeing that the property is kept in good condition.

(4) Seeing that the funds of the church are properly handled.

c. The Official Board will hold a private session each month in which it will endeavor to:

(1) Solve the problems in the church. These decisions shall be presented to the church in session for its approval.

(2) Present a financial report.

(3) Make minutes of the session.

d. The Official Board shall have the oversight of establishing outstations and Sunday Schools in the surrounding district.

e. The Official Board, together with the presbyter of the section, shall extend licenses for lay preachers to those members who are chosen to help the pastor to care for the outstations.

f. The Official Board shall cooperate with the presbyter of the section in arranging for the sectional fellowship meeting.

5. Deaconesses will also be elected by the assembly, or they may be named by the Official Board. There should not be more deaconesses than deacons in an assembly. They will help the pastor in the various activities of the church such as, visiting the sick, keeping the chapel clean and decorated, and in certain cases may form part of the Committee in charge of discipline, when the Official Board requests it.

VII. DEPARTMENTS

There are three organized departments in the local church: The Sunday School, Christ's Ambassadors, and the Women's Missionary Council.

1. These three groups shall have their own officials.

2. They shall work in full harmony with the pastor, who is overseer of all church activities.

3. They may take up offerings for the expenses of their activities.

Bibliography

Gerber, Virgil. *Evangelism/Church Growth.* Pasadena, California: William Carey Library. 1973.

Hodges, Melvin L. *Build My Church.* Springfield, Missouri: Gospel Publishing House. 1957.

.... *A Guide to Church Planting.* Chicago: Moody Press. 1973.

McGavran, Donald. *Church Growth and Christian Mission.* New York: Harper & Row. 1965.

.... *Understanding Church Growth.* Grand Rapids, Michigan: Wm. B. Eerdmans Publishing Co. 1974.

Womack, David. *Breaking the Stained-Glass Barrier.* New York: Harper & Row. 1973.

Yamamori/Lawson, *Introducing Church Growth.* Cincinnatti: Standard Publishing Co.

CHAPTER 1: The Goal of Missions (9-14)

CHAPTER 2: The New Testament Church (15-21)

CHAPTER   3: Self-Government   (22-41)

CHAPTER   4: Self-Propagation   (42-52)

CHAPTER 5: Developing Leadership (53-73)

CHAPTER 6: Self-Support (74-91)

CHAPTER 7: The National Organization (92-98)

CHAPTER 8: Converting to Indigenous Church Methods (99-112)

CHAPTER 9: Hindrances to Conversion to Indigenous Principles (113-120)

CHAPTER 10: Relationship of the Missionary to the
Indigenous Church (121-130)

CHAPTER 11: Pentecost and Indigenous Methods (131-134)

APPENDIX A: Suggested Policy for Missionary Work (135-137)